Translating the Unspeakable

Translating the Unspeakable

Poetry and the Innovative Necessity

essays by

Kathleen Fraser

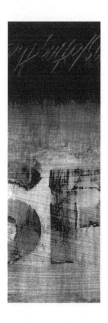

THE UNIVERSITY OF ALABAMA PRESS

Tuscaloosa and London

1 2 3 4 5 6 7 8 9 . 08 07 06 05 04 03 02 01 00

Cover and text design by Shari DeGraw

∞

The paper on which this book is printed meets the minimum requirements of
American National Standard for Information Science–Permanence of Paper for
Printed Library Materials, ANSI Z39.48-1984.

Library of Congress Cataloging-in-Publication Data

Fraser, Kathleen, 1937–
        Translating the unspeakable : poetry and the innovative necessity : essays
/ by Kathleen Fraser.
        p. cm—(Modern and contemporary poetics)
    Includes bibliographical references (p. 207).
    ISBN 0-8173-0989-6 (alk. paper)
    ISBN 0-8173-0990-X (pbk. : alk. paper)
    1. American poetry—Women authors—History and criticism. 2. Women
and literature—United States—History—20th century. 3. American poetry—
20th century—History and criticism. 4. Modernism (Literature)—United
States. I. Title. II. Series.
    PS151 .F75 2000
    811' .5099287—dc21   99-6140

British Library Cataloguing-in-Publication Data available

for Carolyn Burke, Rachel Blau DuPlessis,
Eileen Gregory, Jenny Penberthy,
and Marjorie Perloff

Whose scholarship has helped to provide
a new lens and spine for twentieth-century
women innovative poets

Contents

PART III : Continuum . Contingency . Instability

after.words

Acknowledgments

The essays here collected—some in condensed or considerably revised versions—have previously appeared in the following books and journals. The author expresses her gratitude to those editors who cared enough about the writers and issues discussed to make their pages available to these speculations:

"Things that do not exist without words," *The Wallace Stevens Journal* 17, no. 1 (Spring 1993), editor John N. Serio; and later in a revised version in *Talisman* 9 (Fall 1992), editor Ed Foster.

"The tradition of marginality... and the emergence of *HOW(ever),*" originally published in *FRONTIERS a journal of women studies* 10, no. 3 (1989); republished in revised form in *Where We Stand: Women Poets on Literary Tradition,* edited by Sharon Bryan (New York: W. W. Norton, 1993).

"How did Emma Slide? A matter of gestation" was first published in *Trellis* 3 (1979), editor Maggie Anderson. Later, a revised version appeared in *Feminist Poetics: A Consideration of the Female Construction of Language,* edited by Kathleen Fraser and Judy Frankel (San Francisco, Calif.: University Printing Services, San Francisco State University, 1984).

"Partial local coherence : Regions with illustrations," *Ironwood* 10, no. 2 (Fall 1982), editor Michael Cuddihy.

"Faulty copying," published under the title "This Phrasing Unreliable Except as Here" in *Talisman* 13 (1994).

"Letter from Rome: H.D., Spero, and the reconstruction of gender," *M/E/A/N/I/N/G* 10 (1991), co-editors Mira Shor and Susan Bee.

"Contingent circumstances: Mina Loy > <Basil Bunting," in the essay collection, *Mina Loy: Woman and Poet,* co-edited by Keith Tuma and Maeera Shreiber (Orono, Maine: National Poetry Foundation, 1998).

"Barbara Guest: The location of her," published in *Poetry Flash* (December 1994), editors, Joyce Jenkins and Richard Silberg.

"Line. On the line. Lined up. Lined with. Between the lines. Bottom line." In the essay collection *The Line in Postmodern Poetry,* co-edited by Henry Sayre and Robert Frank (Urbana: University of Illinois Press, 1988).

"'One Hundred and Three Chapters of Little Times': Collapsed and transfigured moments in the cubist fiction of Barbara Guest," in the essay collection *Breaking the Sequence: Women's Experimental Fiction,* co-edited by Miriam Fuchs and Ellen G. Friedman (Princeton, N.J.: Princeton University Press, 1989).

"Translating the Unspeakable: Visual poetics, as projected through Olson's 'field' into current female writing practice" first appeared, in a shorter version, in the anthology *Moving Borders: Three Decades of Innovative Writing by Women,* edited by Mary Margaret Sloan (Jersey City, N.J.: Talisman House, 1998).
    Figures 6–11 in this essay are reprinted from Charles Olson, *The Maximus Poems,* edited by George F. Butterick (Berkeley: University of California Press, 1983), © 1983 The Regents of the University of California. Used by permission.

My particular gratitude goes to the co-curators of this series—Charles Bernstein, who provided me with camaraderie throughout and detailed suggestions for filling in certain histories; and Hank Lazer, whose curiosity and persistent but friendly push persuaded me to assemble this collection. My work has been further supported by the calm hand and thoughtful advice of Assistant Director and Editor-in-Chief, Curtis Clark, and Assistant Managing Editor, Suzette Griffith, both of whom provided clarity and encouragement at critical points. And a bouquet of roses to Jo Ann Wasserman whose wise and thoughtful editorial suggestions saw me through the final stretch.

I am mindful of the artistic support of a small circle of writer friends who, by their examples of fortitude, humor, heart, persistent inquiry, and invention have kept me excited about the not yet finished: David Bromige, Eileen Callahan, Norma Cole, Don Cushman, Adelaide Donnelley, Susan Gevirtz, Robert Glück, Cynthia Hogue, Frances Jaffer, Katharine Ogden, Peter and Meredith Quartermain, Mary-Margaret Sloan, Jo Ann Ugolini, and Peter Weltner — each of whom helped me, in important and discretely different ways, to complete this work.

To Eileen Gregory, whose radiant mind provided me with an unexpectedly useful reading of these essays at a most auspicious moment, I am purely beholden as one is to serendipity.

And, finally, for the model of persistence in tracking inner territories, I am grateful for Arturo, David, and my zany Fraser clan — Ian, Marjorie, Sir James Jeans, Mary, and Anne.

Translating the Unspeakable

Introduction

I've always been moved by the double life and bifurcated sensibility of the classical centaur—human torso grafted onto horse flanks and hooves; or Rene Magritte's reverse mermaid, whose sad fish eyes and barely parted lips rest on dry sand, just beyond waves, mutely grafted to the lower half of a female body . . . unable to utter even a fragment of wariness. In these creatures it is as if the person-centered part of consciousness must be subdued, subjected and destined to remain without voice . . . untranslatable.

Learning to move out from under the perception of non-presence, that uncounted/unwritten part of one's experience; entering into the activity of articulation, attempting this struggle within the inhibiting field of established precedent are urgencies that have shaped the essays here collected.

This writing forms a record of my own uneven passage into that seemingly untouchable world of the already claimed, tracing the moments of access when a particular poet's mysteriously charged words lured me a step further into my own poems.

The public part—the awareness of canon formation with its vagaries of erasure and absolutes of museum installation—came after years of cutting free of my own era's established models of good behavior, writing against and away from prescribed limit and pursuing idiosyncratic models that would give me more room to capture the muted and mutating parts of a partially languaged poem.

•

My particular story is not that unusual for a young woman writer entering the larger literary community in the early Sixties. The books I most often read during that period were those shared by a generation of my peers; the innovative explosion within the visual arts, music, dance, linguistics, philosophy, and political theory had its impact on each of us. By the Seventies, my evolving hybrid poetics—and my former perception of myself as a unique and private (read isolated) poet—began to be shattered by the compelling and unavoidable questions of gender and how these entered one's writing and individual situation in a politicized world. The freedom to explore innovative forms seemed even more necessary and exciting as a condition for the imagination's activity and the architect-poet's expression of that. Yet, it was just around this same time that I began to discover how many exploratory works by modernist women writers had been either quietly removed from anthologies and textbooks . . . or were simply never acknowledged by those empowered to create these documents.

This awareness and witness brought me to troubled silence; but within this stifled place, I began to discover an even more powerful urge to help break down and dismantle the concrete wall. Teaching in three significantly different university writing programs, between 1969 and 1974, underlined that need with increasing urgency. Women students constituted the majority of writers present, but they seldom spoke unless called upon and, in their writing practice, tended to follow a safe and limited model of prosody learned in earlier classes.

It became clear that this performance anxiety—in the charged field of authority and fluency—was not confined to a few "problem" individuals. The inability to enter into public conversation was pervasive. One experienced it in the lopsided post-panel exchanges often held among writers after community literary events: women were seldom heard from. The mandate for a more equitable participation was clear, but the ability to carry it out was waylaid: I, too, was convinced that I did not have the scholarly training required to speak with sufficient authority in public exchanges where writing practice and theory were being tested and defined. Although I valued analytical skills necessary to thinking and writing, I did not feel comfortable pursuing the combative tone that often accompanied the arguments I imagined as necessary to these public exchanges.

This well-defended position began to shift as I immersed myself in the new feminist/modernist scholarship of the Seventies and Eighties and recognized issues and insights that focused and helped to authenticate my own concerns. I began to see how useless an isolationist position could be. I wanted a more concerted acknowledgement of the under-appreciated modernist women innovators, as well as more focus given to the significant body of work being produced by contemporary experimentalist women poets, that is, a two-way street between poets and scholars. But it seemed that this dialogue was not going to happen unless women poets initiated the conversation. Taking on such issues—through the editing of *HOW(ever)* and occasional written talks and essays—became a part of that practice.

•

I began as a poet and it is from this hands-on knowledge of the making of poems that I speak. All my essay writing has been done in response to particular invitations from those who have wished to hear a poet's thinking. There have been instances—as in the Niedecker talk—where the occasion demanded a more thorough and focused reading of current scholarship, without which my own perspective would have been impossible; for these scholarly studies, involving historic fact and critical assessment, I am continuously grateful.

My purpose has *not* been to replicate the useful academic gesture of extended "close readings," except when I was asked to trace the evolution and construction of a particular writer's work—or my own. Instead, I have been interested in the observation of my "cultural moment" in ways that I hoped might extend the reader's understanding of the *necessity* behind the pursuit of innovation; how and why one felt compelled to imagine new terms for the next poem; something that could take one beyond the familiar and well-digested.

In a few cases, I've chosen methods of collage in putting together a jump-cut perspective on a subject, wishing to invite the reader's active participation in making connections. I have wanted to focus and move that attention along a mercurial vector of thought and to allow the comments and details of the different essays to speak to each other and, thus, to reinforce themes touched on more than once.

Thinking about the evolution of this collection, I have been newly struck by the originating French verb *essayer* and several of its possible meanings: to try; to test, or run trials on; to try one's hand at (*s'essayer*). In one way or another, the entering of a genre never imagined as "mine" has been a dare, a testing, a trying on and a learning to trust an entirely different method of discursive investigation, while embracing the more intuitive jumps invited by poetry—my first language.

Part I

Auto . Bio . Poetics

September 7

Dear Narcissus,

Is language, in fact, the pool? Looking into your words as if they represented a surface of water (Narcissus gazes with longing, trying to find himself), do I then find me, a word I know? Yes. No. Some deflection, inflexing of where we might overlap. Sitting on your lap, a word comes back at me, as an echo. So I divest myself of the disembodied me. Echo is She who watches Narcissus look for himself and returns him to himself, slightly altered, by her very attentiveness.

Where am I?

Love,

Echo

(KF, "Notes re: Echo," 1980)

Things that do not exist without words

Remember how the crickets came
Out of their mother grass, like little kin,
In the pale nights, when your first imagery
Found inklings of your bond to all that dust.

—Stevens, "Le Monocle de Mon Oncle"

What lost language first awakened her and soothed her to sleep? As early as she could remember, Harry Lauder's brisk Scottish tenor floated up the stairs on dark, snowy mornings . . . later it was an Italian coloratura when the weather turned warm. Always at 7:30 A.M., the radio's tense male voice, like the bark of a dog, quoted farm prices from Chicago, and at 8 a rousing march boomed against her ear.

After breakfast, the dishes cleared, her father would read: "Though I speak with the tongues of men and of angels, and have not love, I am become as sounding brass, or a tinkling cymbal." She and her brother repeated the language of King James into memory. At lunch, she begged for nonsense: "Jabberwocky," songs from *Through the Looking-Glass*, Edward Lear limericks—little fables packed with sound and! Silliness:"There was an old man of St. Bees / Who thought he was stung by a wasp," etc. Gaiety spread across her father's face, no matter how many times he repeated it. Unrelieved responsibilities disappeared for a little—bills to be paid, Sunday's sermon yet to write."Reason's click-clack" was replaced by the pure joy of "accurate song."

(These memories do not exist without words.)

FRAME: First delivered as a talk to the Wallace Stevens symposium held in 1991 at the Modern Language Association meetings in San Francisco, where three poets—Robert Hass, Robert Mezey, and myself—were asked to speak about our relation as writers to the poetry of Stevens. This essay later appeared in the *Wallace Stevens Journal* 17, no. 1 (Spring 1993), and in a somewhat revised version in *Talisman* 9 (Fall 1992).

Surrounded by utterance, both common and uncommon, song entered the child's ear and defined her, an ever-present page lightly penciled with the graph of her own uneven movement into personhood.

Then it was the first day of school. And when the seventh day arrived, all doors to playfulness slammed shut. In seventh grade, Miss Elsie Foote began to teach Poetry Lessons. What had been joyful became flattened and restrictive. *Do Not Sit On The Grass.* Acts of terrorism reigned: four large pages of the slow, sleepy prelude to Longfellow's "Evangeline" would be committed to memory and recited by each student in front of the class. Poetry's instruction soon undermined that early appetite for words; there was, instead of pleasure, the considerable question of getting it right. She was kept after school, shamed for her refusal, the last in the class to commit it to memory. She who had by now stopped listening was, in any case, a most inappropriate girl in "a most unpropitious place."

Wallace Stevens believed that poets were born. What does it mean, to be born a poet, to be borne into poetic language as if the mind were waiting like a large empty page to be imprinted with the intaglio markings of a world crowding forward to make its impress? Is it a genetic propensity, a particular magnetic pull toward the rhythms and clinks of assonance and dissonance? Is it the fortune of close exposure to syllable's infinite capacity for musical charge? Is the ground prepared in discretionary ways so that a particular child, opening into adolescent consciousness, hears the self multiplying, and needs to capture and free it? Surely, exposure to the "brillig, slithy toves" of Lewis Carroll's "Jabberwocky," or Hopkins's "rosemoles all in stipple upon trout that swim" ("Pied Beauty"), Dickinson's "and Doges—surrender—/ Soundless as dots—on a Disc of Snow—"or Wallace Stevens's "Complacencies of the peignoir, and late / Coffee and oranges in a sunny chair" are cause for ecstatic response . . . if the mind's ear has been tuned.

We are summoned into the physiology of listening by our mother's heartbeat and the rude squall of our own arrival. If we survive, that listening develops into a sweeter capacity and the maternal "rou-cou-cou" and "Ti-tum-tum-tum" is soon nestling close to our ear, luring us into the beginnings of relation.

Recalling my own early listening during pre-school years, I seek some clue or reconstruction of who it was that found herself borne up into the untranslatable elation of a Wallace Stevens poem. Who was she, this listener at some improvised after-class party in the early Sixties, suddenly dropped into unexplored chambers of feeling by a fugitive music that entered and *made* its claim? The once radiant page of the mind, for years normalized into standard-size foolscap, was again destabilized, its tactile surface brought alive, as if with the marks and artful fabrication of handmade paper.

·

"Ramon Fernandez, tell me, if you know. . . ." In someone's front room across from the Eighth St. Bookstore in Greenwich Village, two young men have been reciting together the final passages of "The Idea of Order at Key West." Their eyes are shy, shining, not quite looking at each other. They want to share this moment, yet to keep communion — each with his private place in which the poem's words continue to resonate. They have read beyond fashion or obligation. They have traveled outside of habit and into the currents of their own responsiveness.

"Ecstasy etymologically derives from the Greek *ekstasis,* from *ex,* 'out,' plus *histanai,* 'to place.' Thus, it means something like 'placed out.' Ecstasy is when you are no longer within your own frame: some sort of going outside takes place" (Gallop 1988, 152).

She takes her monthly lunch allowance and buys *The Collected Poems of Wallace Stevens,* and spends the noon hour in her office cubicle transfixed:

> I placed a jar in Tennessee,
> And round it was, upon a hill.
> It made the slovenly wilderness
> Surround that hill.
> (Stevens 1961, 76)

Jar and hill, never consciously present, are now suggested. Static of world subsides. The listener, until this moment amnesiac, grows attentive in the wilderness of her partial formation. But there is a double thrill. While his

words shed light, they also resonate with inarticulate mystery. She becomes fascinated by how this happens, how a particular diction is constructed to surprise the mind's dumb regularity.

She reads:

> I was the world in which I walked, and what I saw
> Or heard or felt came not but from myself;
> And there I found myself more truly and more strange.
>
> (65)

She understands, if primitively, that those half-formed words ghosting
through her *are* her—"[come] not but from [her] self"—and that this
unfinished self, this "strangeness," might begin to commit itself to paper.

She reads:

> Chieftain Iffucan of Azcan in caftan
> Of tan with henna hackles, halt!
>
> (75)

The walls of her cubicle give way; her father's voice chants pure nonsense.
She reads on:

> imperative haw
> Of hum, inquisitorial botanist,
> And general lexicographer of mute
> And maidenly greenhorns . . .
>
> (28)

Each poem has moved her beyond the familiar frame of a day's mechanical response. Bland unthinking becomes, for these moments, muscular. Thought is musically defined. She's a field charged with sound. The
page begins revising its surface.

•

I have been talking about the long summons into the vocation of poetry,
the mysterious yet concrete process of self-recognition that was—and con-

tinues to be—crystallized for me in the work of Stevens. He brings to poetry's vocation the essential gift: the unequaled pleasure of reinventing one's idiom—that secret encoding of self's journey that supersedes a narcissistic, simple-minded lexicon of the "confessional" or a quickly depleted vocabulary of commonality. Instead, he clarifies the poet's role as antenna and inventor/namer of subtle swift sightings that remain absent until caught in words.

Rilke speaks of this calling in his ninth "Duino Elegy":

> Perhaps we are *here* in order to say: house,
> bridge, fountain, gate, pitcher, fruit-tree, window—
> at most: column, tower. . . . But to *say* them, you must understand,
> oh to say them *more* intensely than the Things themselves ever dreamed of existing.
> (Rilke, trans. Mitchell, 1995)

In a 1981 interview in the Italian literary journal *leggere,* the Syrian poet Adonis proposed a distinction Stevens would have liked regarding naming and poetic language:

> In Arabic, things have a multiplicity of names. Let's take the names of elements belonging to the material sphere, such as "earth," "dust" or "rain." To each of these elements corresponds forty names. And what belongs to the conceptual sphere, such as "exploration," "knowledge" or "ignorance" can in turn often be designated by at least thirty names. . . . The name does not designate the wholeness of the thing, but only one of its aspects; the thing, therefore, is an ensemble of situations and aspects, an ensemble of words.
>
> The word is essentially a token and the poet writes with token-words. As a consequence, for the Arab sensibility, language is not language by virtue of its referent. But on the other hand, the thing is not a thing but by grace of the word that names it. It's not that language "descends" toward things, but that things "ascend"

or aspire toward language, which poeticizes them. As if a thing
might not exist except through locutions, or as if it might acquire
presence only as it is interwoven with language or transformed
into language.

(trans. A. K. Bierman)

It is this aspiration to locution that Stevens articulates, this lyric pressure
of the moment's assembled meanings that makes up his rendering of sensibility in flux. It is the construction of what he discovers and how he
knows, through attentive observation, multiplied by the sound and veloc-
ity of what he imagines. His mind, "in the act of finding / What will
suffice," discovers a perpetual motion on the page and, for these reasons, is
never caught in the fixed date of attitude or event. With this description
before one, it is particularly troubling—from a working poet's perspective,
as well as a reader's—to note the narrow reception of *Harmonium* in 1923,
remembering the enormous excitement upon my first reading of these
poems in 1961, almost forty years after its publication. I believed, then, that
I understood Stevens utterly, though I couldn't have necessarily articulated
the why and how of my ecstatic lift-off. For example, how did I read "Thirteen Ways of Looking at a Blackbird" at that time? It represented, I thought,
early cubist perspective—seeing and hearing from the invented vantage
of thirteen discrete planes, instead of going along with the singleness of a
common, unitary perception, a "first idea." It was about refreshing one's
capacity to imagine the world through the artist's ability—"to subvert the
tyranny of old orders"—the blackbird, buried in the false bottom of the
top hat, pulled forth . . . and pulled forth again.

Now I read that poem, with no less magic, but I hear its darker message
as well. I see it not only as a tour de force of imagining, but also as a series
of warnings signaling the inevitability of error, the flaw that waits patiently
to undo one's "idea of order," the continuous hover of what we would
have preferred to avoid. Although Stevens intended each stanza as a kind
of Mallarméan state of the soul, I think he'd find validity in both these
other readings.

Reviewing early criticism of *Harmonium,* I believe that his judges were
too quickly seduced by what Stevens liked to call his gaudy surface and

not sufficiently cognizant of the darker intentions, the structural under-pinnings so evident to us. Harriet Monroe once rejected new poems of his, calling them "recondite, erudite, provocatively obscure, with a kind of modern, gargoyle grin in them,"—a perfect list, apparently, of exactly what attracted me to them in 1961. Gorham Munson put a pejorative spin on Stevens's irrepressible resuscitation of English by calling him "the first dandy of American letters."

John Gould Fletcher warned: "I make bold to say that Mr. Stevens is the most accomplished and not one of the least interesting of modern Ameri-can poets. But for the future, he must face a clear choice of evils: he must either expand his range to take in more of human experience, or give up writing altogether. *Harmonium* is a sublimation which does not permit of sequel" (quoted in Bates 1985, 124). The authoritarian ring of "he must either/or" and "which does not permit" sounds a little like Miss Elsie Foote, in seventh grade. We know, however, that Stevens worried about these questions and, for the most part, gave up publishing for nearly ten years after this public scolding. The ability to survive such drubbing should not go unremarked, nor the "zebra leaves" nor the "gramaphoons" that followed, both because and in spite of it.

I like to think of Wallace Stevens walking through the vast park that separated his house from the Hartford Insurance Company. It seems such an austere and unexotic wilderness, compared to the "green freedom of a cockatoo" or the "sultriest fulgurations flickering" before the imagined eyes of an imagined "he" sitting in an imagined "Naples," writing home about it. The concept of the "local" was so important to him; he was al-most envious of what he saw as certain friends' authentic otherness, rooted in tropical specificity and slightly foreign vernacular. And yet, though he took small trips, especially to the South, he almost never chose to travel beyond the United States. He loved the company of his own mind most. Living there, he could—in a sense—have it all, entertaining every possi-bility of action and diction with the fullest liberty. Walking the two miles of Elizabeth Park, eyes turned inward, he cultivated the flora and fauna of language and produced uncommon graftings.

As if my own genetic codes had been researched with sudden cunning by the great botanist of language—and dozens of latent capacities newly identified—I was stunned by my most recent encounter with Stevens. Yet *again* I was unloosed from ordinary habits of reading, transported into the ecstatic, remembered and renamed by his music as I read—verified and marked by the "henna hackles," the "ric-a-nic," the "clearing opalescence" of his language. I found that all the old favorites remained passionately alive in my mind, each *again* the first love whose startling mystery evoked new self-knowledge and intense responsiveness—recognizing things that do not, cannot have existed without his words to locate them.

To book as in to foal. To son.

1. monologue

Catching two words. Pulling apart and rePasting a paragraph on the same night spiders crowd and come pushing out from the closet door at the actual child.

Working in the next room without knowing this, to hear him tell of it years later and to hold this. Nights of long fear.

To sorrow the poem, to sorrow and tear at its lines, to open its vein. Looking for blue. Expecting it.

Instead, to find red. Scar tissue. Long hollow empty place. Quill of a feather.

Writing lines, watching lines elasticize and tatter, not knowing how to solace the dark, child's eyes open/eyes awake, with mind yet struck in infant night-terror. An otherness you know nothing of. Can you put this? Can you hold it quietly?

Deferral. To other's book.

FRAME: This piece was originally written for a forthcoming collection of essays, *New Writings on Motherhood and Poetics,* co-edited by Patricia Dienstfrey and Brenda Hillman. The need for further attention to this subject was made evident by a related conference on "Artists and Motherhood: Work, Identity and Creation," held in the spring of 1996 at New College, San Francisco, and sponsored by Small Press Distribution.

To work at night to work when child is sleeping, is drawing. Each chore that wants you. Assignments marked. To unplug the phone on Sunday when the child is with his father, to not answer a knock, to put away the folders of others, other's book, put away feeding. To sit in the chair in silence. To place suddenly urgent books on the cleared oak table, to touch the new notebook, to open it at the blank page; lines on the page that mark emptiness. To feel the lines recovering one, into them. Falling into the page. Away from every other.

To book as in to foal. To son. Those first wobbly legs. To have this actual child. To try to show him how to stand up. The two of them now, instead of the three of them, yet not deleting the father. Being without him now.

The father at the door on Saturday

or the father with the actual child between them, swinging him along, and then . . . then the actual child comes home. The poem comes home. She is home.

Through necessity's trap door. To be with other poets (mothers, among them) sitting in a basement room, ones who can barely speak yet must write. Can sometimes reach into their own & private horde. But some cannot speak because cannot lift out the sleek word into this sudden formal classroom air. Broken thoughtline chatter and humility. Interrupted minute. Someone's daughter is zipped shut but writing inside of that. You hear her trying. Trying to put it right. Tight squeeze through these neat and tidy lines. Lanes. Starting gate's official gun. The poem leaning forward. Taut. Not to swing away. To allay fear.

Look at her. In arrears. Delayed.
Taught. To frustration.

To wake up and know the body is dead. To notice the air is bright but the body is not. To substitute little trays of food with cut animal shapes of sandwich, baked cookies, and mother cake with mother chocolate, stories before sleep, "this little piggy went to market," hands rubbing his feet. To sing: *A grasshopper hopped on a redbud tree / and said "Come away, come away with me. Come awaaayyy, come awaaayyy.* To lower the light.

Then to fall into the saved book, her own bed and again to be called back into the dark. Hark, the spider's interruption.

Book gone, song again. The mother is singing as her mother sang, putting the sound in her. Now she rocks him or is a bird and does not know who is who.

Then remembers the weight of the first little book her father gave her, with a father's silly drawing inside it, bird named ODAROLOC standing on one foot, leg long, head hidden under wing. Now the bird appears again, in sleep. In its beak an empty book. She opens it.

To book again, to son. To teach him *al dente* pasta and first-pressed oil, the garlic and parsley tossed in. Not to be helpless, yet to weep helplessly in front of him, not to dissemble. To choose this particular quill for making shapes and marks. To give him that dropped feather. A crayon, a brush and paint, a wall of paper endlessly unrolling. To give him red and blue jars of thick paste color. His hands in it and the brushes making their mark.

To admire and want. To want to say, but feel chagrin for obvious saying, but to be urgent, defying, pinning together and sewing, to be ripping apart and wiping, to be cooking soup and typing, often to be starting and not finishing, but to be planting in the garden with him, watering and digging, watching for the spider, but to be edited out, but "to submit" and to be "rejected," but to choose a desk and a chair and to feel the singleness of it, the actual child of it coming home.

The child howling with hunger of her, anger at her going out the door, not wanting the others to take her, but pushing her away from him (her coming in the door for him). Himself unto himself. More himself.

Then her feet shod with shoes to be danced, coming and going, saying "Look how we work beside each other," she with her hollow door desk and he with his solid child desk. They make pictures and cross out words and everything is in pieces all over the desk and the floor and scribbled over pages drawn to their edges with Spiderman moonwalks, weaponry inventories . . . whatever is needed.

To have this actual son in this child. To try to explain absence, the two of them now, or often a different three of them. Flying out of his sightlines. The book of her and the foal of him without deferring to one of them. To find this peculiar path and follow its constant changing. To sit alone at the table. To revise a passive construction. To choose the ticking body parts and the knocking poem unable to speak. To talk to it. To mother it.

Violets the lover in her wants and is given . . . and the child is also given plastic models and metal toys whose hooks and claws soon break. But he glues together parts of monsters that don't fit the cheaply printed instructions. He unfolds hybrids. Nobody tells him how, his being a child and curious. And used to glueing.

To get lost, then to look for the true pact between them, teaching herself the motherpart, how to think and to learn that grammar of his lengthening. To revise. To leave him alone. To worry. To give him a push. To book, to foal, to write partial sentences. Hiding her worrying. To glue each sentence together with parts of its making. To have written the sentence's smooth beauty and, later, to break it apart.

To let the poem pour from the closet, long erratic music-tugging lines and word horde of the broken-in-on nightlight.

To tango.
To monster.
To let the lover into the mother world.

And that boy, what a boy, what a gorgeous boy, what a soul in that boy, what a poem in that boy.

interval

"The pen runs along the page like a seismograph, its motion alternately evoking large, ominous crags and thin, immaterial crests which run, uphill and down, across an otherwise white page like notes on some monumental orchestral score" (Micheal Gibson, "The Landscapes of Raffi Kaiser," *International Herald Tribune*).

2. dialogue

A: So what do you think?
B: About what?

A: About the monologue.
B: I was glad for the last line.

A: What do you mean?
B: Your story was so sad, otherwise.

A: Sad? Maybe sometimes. . . . but mostly we were just trying to figure out how to find what we needed, being two strong individuals and such a tiny family. We were in the car a lot, in the summers. I remember the red rock canyons; he took pictures of the dinosaur statuary. Sacred Indian places, country music on the radio, dust storms. We always had a cat or two, wherever we lived. He would name them for how they looked — Gum-camel, Witchy, Watermelon. And then Maynard kept coming from over the back fence and finally stayed, completely devoted to him.

He liked to wander loose in malls, I preferred friends' kitchens. We both liked museums and Chinese food, camping-out for awhile and then, after a few nights, thick white towels and TV. Once we woke up to a bear prowling in the next campsite . . .

B: Hmmm. . . .

A: Why hmmm? Do you mean I shouldn't talk about those times?

B: I just don't see the point of writing about it.

A: But it's part of how we grew up. Side by side. Looking back, I think it was a pretty good model — showing him how to "work," by stealing time to do my own. I was close-by. That wasn't sad. What was sad was each of us losing someone out of our daily lives, someone we loved and needed. One way or another it happens, but ideally not so soon in a person's life. But he didn't lose me and I didn't lose him. He helped me to pay close attention. I learned to let him grow up. We both had our own long journeys going on inside us. Whenever we hung out together — especially in the car, when the motion seemed to loosen us up — we had some great talks. And laugh! Sometimes I had to stop the car. But when he was drawing he was often in planetary space, whereas when I was writing I was attaching myself to the page as if I were driving or drawing all over it.

B: But in the story, the child seems to be an obstacle . . .

A: You mean, to the writing? Everything was an obstacle. That was part of the problem of trying to write *outside* of a vacuum — that is, to have always imagined the poem as something that could be written *only* inside perfect, uninterrupted time, an air-tight vacuum: quiet. Waiting for the day when this moment would finally arrive. But everything kept breaking-in on continuity; everyone wanted your attention, if you were a mother. Each person imagined he or she was the only one. Apparently the maternal image is in there, pulsing pure neon. You could be carrying a dozen other lives inside you waiting to unfold. But it seems unavoidable, this leaning toward motherlove. This wanting to be held and listened to. This continuous presence of expectation.

B: You mean signed and sealed in the genes?

A: Or the years of someone before you, showing you. . . . I don't know.
B: I never had trouble like that. I could just sit in the frontroom and write, with the kids playing and their friends tearing in and out.

A: Not me. I wanted a door. I had to get completely closed-off from someone else's waiting and needing. It kept hovering. The phone was always ringing. You wanted to be available, to be a generous person. Especially to your actual child. But the milk kept running out, so it was off to Safeway again, instead of to the desk. I'd hear something starting up inside my brain, trying to get out—even just the *desire* to think *anything,* to find words for it, move them around on the page . . . and I'd run for a pen and begin, but it was mostly disruption and intervention, arguments and pardons, hugs and little cups of custard meant to last a few days in the fridge.

Time kept running out. You could either stop and cook or point at the refrigerator and fight the guilt. And always there was something new to track down, to keep that child's mind open and flexible and muscular, to honor its curiosity and persistence . . . (but oh, the tedium of playgrounds and birthday parties . . . my god, the chat could drive you to the edge!). I used to wince when I heard men—usually writer types—talking about "the abyss" . . . as if it were an immense set of cosmic jaws lying in wait, in some abstract future oblivion. Whereas, I felt that darkness hovering around the corner, almost every normal day. And I *knew* what it was. It was the bleakness and frustration of no time alone, no free path into the forest, no access.

It was the problem of feeling trapped with no way out . . . feeling one had lost one's hold on an authentic self. I mean, if a writer can't find time to make notes and shape the perceptions and voices unravelling inside her, she can get very crazy. Most of the time, it was just the two of us and somehow that made for more interruptions than less. And of course there were the problems of earning a living—dentist bills, the car payment and the mortgage—thinking ahead, before sleep, about the next morning, the order of what must be done to get us both to school on time::his day, my day, his night, my night.

Meanwhile, art supplies, guitar strings, Star Trek uniform . . . only one certain color and fabric would do. The riding boots were researched for weeks. The kid's mind was avid. He loved beautiful things, quite particular things, and TV junk-hype and the terrifying, invented stuff he made up in his drawing books. Food and objects gave him a safety zone, proof of having enough of his own . . . that I would be there, through any question and every sorrow, to help him figure out his turf.

B: You didn't *have* to do all that . . .

A: But I *wanted* to . . . Except for writing, I was probably happiest in those moments, helping him feel taken care of and safe . . . yet, later, torn with guilt anyway, worrying I'd never done enough for him . . . or for me.

B: If you were enjoying it so much, why the grief? Why couldn't you just accept being a mother, since that's what you'd chosen . . . I mean, how many books do you need to write to make you feel o.k.?

A: It's not a question of numbers, some abstract measurement of accomplishment. It's really about survival . . . how one stays alive to one's private art, one's particular connection to being and making something new out of—okay—the life you've chosen, but also what is choosing you. How do you stay alive to that? By working. Alone in your workspace. If you are a writer, you *must* write. To only think about it, and wish for it, without sitting down to do it, is to deny your gift, to damp it down. Either way, the muscle of the mind atrophies and the intimacy of one's relation to one's work (the *pleasure* of doing it) diminishes proportionately. Self-diminishment is painful. Poor mother, poor child—they both feel its effects.

I *had* to find a way to write. Writing was different than loving him or working for us or all the big and little shifts of fiction and passing romance that kept going on above and below the life of me and him and of writing. Loving and writing and earning a living were the priorities. I had to find time enough for all three or I felt I would not survive. Bottom line. Still, my students kept arriving for conferences. Their manuscripts and mid-terms piled-up on my writing desk. The weekends were entirely eaten up by being useful and resourceful. Necessity. Consolation. Transportation. One day it hit me. It wasn't going to stop. There wasn't going to be the perfect vacuum of silence and continuity. So I had to invent another way to capture the poems—a place I could walk into and back out of. Trust with a phrase or a sentence. Accretion of parts, maps of disruption.

B: But what about beauty and form?

A: Beauty, as I'd been taught to think of it, no longer interested me in the same way.

B: I really don't see . . .

A: . . . how you can write a poem without it, right?

B: Right.

A: I had to keep my eye on things. I had to remember for two. The old idea of "beauty" no longer served—neither the question, nor the answer. My thoughts were blips and scrolls and departures. The task was to catch them just as they came up to the surface. Unexpectedness, chaos, pressures, and breaks. Everything seemed to tilt, to barely maintain itself. In spite of all effort. I thought, why not write that way? While the beautiful, seamless poem stopped being relevant to my own way of working, the open field of the page became more and more compelling. That mark of a seismograph across an empty score.

interval

gestation: (1) the act of carrying young in the womb from conception to delivery (2) the development of a plan in the mind. (*Webster's Unabridged Dictionary,* Second edition)

3. pedagogy

Catching two words . . . pulling apart and rePasting . . . to tear at its lines, to open . . . watching lines elasticize . . . recovering one . . . often to be starting and not finishing . . . and scribbled over pages drawn to their edges . . . to find this peculiar path and follow its constant changing . . . to choose the ticking body parts and the knocking poem unable to speak . . . to talk to it . . . to glue each sentence together with parts of its making . . . to have written the sentence's smooth beauty and, later, to break it apart . . .
to let the poem pour from the closet, long erratic music-tugging lines and word horde of the broken-in-on nightlight.

—for David, 5/30/1997

The tradition of marginality . . .
and the emergence of *HOW(ever)*

On the outside, you attempt to conform to an order which is alien to you. Exiled from yourself, you fuse with everything you encounter. You mime whatever comes near you. You become whatever you touch. In your hunger to find yourself, you move indefinitely far from yourself. . . . Assuming one model after another, one master after another, changing your face, form and language according to the power that dominates you. Sundered . . .

— Luce Irigaray, "When Our Lips Speak Together"

As a representative of purity, moral, ideological, intellectual, or anything else, I am a walking lie. My own work and that of the women I admire gives its allegiance to the messiness of experience.

— Nina Auerbach, "Engorging the Patriarchy"

Radium's radioactivity was so great that it could not be ignored. It seemed to contradict the principle of conservation of energy and thereby forced a reconsideration of the foundation of physics.

— *Encyclopedia Britannica*

When I was in second grade, my Aunt Dottie came to visit. She was a tall, glamorous brunette who worked as an executive secretary for Western Union. She smoked cigarettes and had no husband or children. These things immediately defined her in my mind as a separate category of female from my mother who, as the wife of a Presbyterian minister and mother of four closely spaced children, represented to me a world of benevolent oppres-

FRAME: This essay was first delivered in 1985 at The Poetry Project at St. Marks Church, New York, N.Y., as part of a talk series — with the same name — curated by Charles Bernstein. It was subsequently published in *FRONTIERS a journal of women studies* [*A Special Issue: Women and Words*] 10, no. 3 (1989), and later in the anthology, *Where We Stand: Women Poets on Literary Tradition*, edited by Sharon Bryan (New York: W. W. Norton, 1993).

sion. While Aunt Dottie rested and bathed before dinner, we children had to be quiet because this was her vacation. Each night she appeared at our modest dining table in her long, red velvet dressing gown, trailing perfume and powder.

For me, the single most powerful event of her two-week stay was the evening she took my mother and me off to the movies to see *Madame Curie,* starring Greer Garson, at the Orpheum Theatre in downtown Tulsa. We arrived in the late, dim afternoon, but when we emerged the world was dark and sharp with perspective. We were taken to a fancy restaurant for club sandwiches and chocolate sodas, and what followed was probably my first conversation with women about possibility and probability.

Madame Curie has been described by a contemporary of hers as "a pale, timid little woman in black cotton dress, with the saddest face I had ever looked upon." But Greer Garson's face—a study in curiosity, humor, intelligence, and determination—will always take Curie's visual place in my mind. It was to Garson's face and Curie's quest that I turned, increasingly hooked as she lived out her life on screen, searching for that element which had not yet been imagined or named.

In the movie, Madame Curie has obstacle after obstacle to surmount, including the overwhelming disdain of the all-male French scientific community. Her arduous tasks are on the scale of Psyche's, as she sorts through a ton of pitchblende to come up with one-tenth of a gram of uncontaminated radium chloride. The tension builds through endless failures in the lab, as she uses what has been proposed by traditional scientific method thus far, then finally discards it to consult the further reaches of her imagination for what might work. Halfway through the film, her husband, Pierre, who has worked side by side with her, is killed in a street accident, and she is left alone and grief-stricken. Still, she persists in her obsession, spending long hours in the lab, even though the pads of her thumbs are growing numb from the powerful effects of the radioactive substance.

Everything now seems to be in black and white. She spends endless days and nights sitting before the microscope, trying this solution and that, with no sign of significant results. Then one night, in exhaustion, she returns to the lab to check her experiments and before she can turn on the light she sees a faint glow coming from one of the saucers where her chemical solutions are waiting. It is radium giving off that light. It is the glowing evidence that she has been seeking. It is like nothing that has come before it. It has eluded her for years. Curie finds, ultimately, that unlike phosphorescence, radium is not dependent upon an outside source of energy but appears to arise spontaneously from the uranium itself—an unheard-of departure from the known laws of nature.

I remembered this image when talking with a friend about our first female role models. I realized that mine was Madame Curie, looking for the imagined light in the dark of her lab. There weren't a lot of women role models after that, certainly not among the poets I was taught. The few samples of ladylike grace offered up in junior high school were not for me. I wrote a bit of doggerel and a bit more of private seriousness, but essentially I had been well-trained to fear poetry. I resented its refusal to give over any meanings other than those few handed down by my teachers. My career plan was to be a journalist. I graduated with B.A. in English literature from Occidental, a reputable liberal arts college where we read the great works of literature and philosophy and heard lectures on "The History of Civilization" every morning for two years running, delivered in the college chapel where we all were seated next to each other on long polished wooden pews, taking notes or writing comments and sending them down the row.

In these years, there were no women-authored texts on the reading list. This absence had its effect and made its point subliminally clear. Several of my women friends began writing poetry and would pass along their new poems during the more boring lectures. Thus poetry actively reentered my life through my peers—a kind of resistance movement going on in the third row; suddenly it seemed intriguing. Within a year, I found myself writing something resembling poems. I would type my final drafts sitting on the floor of the girls' shower room late at night so as not to disturb my roommate, then rush to Civ. lecture to send my first efforts down the chapel pew and back.

For my birthday, junior year, my friends gave me T. S. Eliot's *Collected Poems,* William Carlos Williams's *Journey to Love,* e.e. cummings's *A Miscellany,* and Federico García Lorca's *Selected Poems.* I felt deeply shy and thrilled. My barely emerging identity was being acknowledged with this act of recognition. I soon switched majors from philosophy to English literature but very little of that study included modern poetry; certainly, there were no women poets discussed. When I graduated, I did not know of the work of Marianne Moore or H.D. or Gertrude Stein . . . although it's true that they were not English. I somehow got hold of Virginia Woolf on my own and was pulled further into poetry by reading *The Waves*.

My first poems tried to model themselves on what I was reading—the dark presentiments of Eliot, the surreal lyrics of Lorca and a few sudden untranslatable intensities inspired by Dylan Thomas. I tried to effect an e.e. cummings homage without it looking too derivative. I was deeply attracted by his refusal to conform to the conventional syntax and grammar of acceptable mainstream poetry. Cummings's passionate resistance would align itself in my mind with Madame Curie's refusal to give up her belief in the possibility of a new element. Already, I was aware that I carried a number of clamoring voices in me, arguing, protesting, obsessively repeating themselves . . . my mind was polyphonic and fragmenting, as I heard it, split between my resolve to be an attractive and acceptable female student, and my stubborn resistance to all rules—including those of prosody, which did not appear to describe my hesitant and multiple ways of perceiving and forming thought. All was shifting ground and formally suspect.

Soon after graduation, I left to pursue my career in journalism in New York City where I eventually met several budding poets who suggested I join a writing workshop. One woman, a poet who signed her manuscripts G. Oden to prevent sexist prejudgment of her work, invited me to a reading given by Stanley Kunitz. I was thrilled by his Yeatsian language and passionate metaphysical vision and signed up for his poetry workshop at the YMHA Poetry Center (later The 92nd Street Y), learning through him to admire the splendid work of Elizabeth Bishop. I also acquired the skills to write a certain kind of good poem, of which I sold three to *The New Yorker*, several years later. During this workshop period, we began hearing of Sylvia Plath through Kunitz and Robert Lowell. In the autumn of 1962 we were listening to her poems; by 1963, she was dead. Plath was my first female role model in poetry. The male poets and editors were in love with her. Lowell read her poems at his own readings. Not only did she have the superb craft and ear, but there was clearly something seductive for the literary world in her tragic end.

It turned out that there *were* a few other women writing poetry. In the early Sixties, I happened upon several wonderfully intelligent poems by Adrienne Rich in *The Nation*. In 1963, I heard of a two-week summer workshop being taught by a woman poet—Daisy Alden. I decided to spend my vacation studying with her, although I'd seen only random poems. Something in me yearned for a teacher who could—by her work and presence—show how one might attempt to be in the world, as a woman poet, without succumbing to nervous breakdown, total isolation, or suicide as a solution.

When I arrived at the workshop, we were told that Daisy Alden was sick and that our teacher would be Kenneth Koch. Koch was on the attack; he cut down any sign of high seriousness or emotional vulnerability in the person or the poem. I recovered from him the playful attitude toward poetic language that I'd loved in my father's recitations of Lewis Carroll and various nonsense verse; also, we were taught a certain skepticism toward sentimental poetic retreads. That was healthy.

Through Koch, I met Frank O'Hara and through O'Hara, Barbara Guest, whose poetry and person Frank admired enormously. While O'Hara's energetic celebration of the whole of life in its dailiness was a great permission-giver, it was Guest's linguistic mysteries that finally lingered in my imagination, composed and collaged from the precise fragments of her painterly witness and her skeptical wariness of language's confinement and over-simplification. Barbara Guest was the only woman poet named in the first generation of the New York School. In 1970, when the second generation of the New York School emerged, full of ego and ambition, a major anthology of the works of the New York School came out edited by David Shapiro (around twenty-three at the time) and Ron Padgett (in his late twenties). Barbara Guest, a major figure in the painting and poetry scene throughout the Fifties and Sixties, publishing her poems and art criticism in many New York magazines and reading on various New York School programs—by then, author of three poem collections and one monograph on the painter Robert Goodnough—was left out of the anthology. Meanwhile, twenty-six men were included—some of them brilliant poets such as Edwin Denby and James Schuyler, others merely adequate camp followers. The anthology included one woman, Bernadette Mayer, a young experimentalist from the third generation. Guest's erasure was my first in-person encounter with this common historic practice.

Through the Sixties, various movements emerged and ran parallel courses, all sharing two observable similarities. They each had male theorists setting forth the new aesthetic dogma, usually asserted in published correspondence or theoretical repudiation of others' existing poetics. Each poetics constellation or school had its token woman poet.

Few established women writers seemed interested in helping to change that ratio. It was not difficult to see that there was only so much room for women at the top. Under the fatherly aegis of W. C. Williams and Robert Duncan, Denise Levertov's poems received serious critical attention. Anne Sexton followed Plath—watched over by Robert Lowell—baffling East Coast critics who were intrigued and appalled by her confessions of emotional instability. Among West Coast writers around Jack Spicer and Gary Snyder, Joanne Kyger was acknowledged—if minimally. Diane DiPrima, as sister figure of the Beats, was known for publishing many knowns and unknowns in her mimeo magazine, *Floating Bear.* Gwendolyn Brooks represented a token black academic tradition, but her work was not widely known or taught in the white community; Carolyn Kizer, under Kunitz's mentorship, was admired for her finely pitched, celebratory lyric verse, but her major poetic satire, "Pro Femina," was not sufficiently appreciated until a later generation. Adrienne Rich won a Yale Younger Poet's prize and often appeared in the aesthetic company of W. S. Merwin and Galway Kinnell. Muriel Ruykeyser appeared to stand alone, a kind of high priestess chanting her visionary works. The idea that very few women wrote poetry was still popularly accepted.

This list is, of course, an oversimplification, but it is a kind of topological map of certain formations that were clear enough to be noticed. There *were* others, innocently conspiring in their own *non*recognition. We literary women had all been taught our manners and, with few exceptions in the Sixties, women writers sent out their work and waited to be taken up by powerful male editors and mentors who were willing to discover them and authenticate their reality as writers. Women mentors and editors were in very short supply, still captured by their own tentative power base.

One might speculate that such neglect gave women poets a kind of freedom from the confines of public approval and aesthetic directive to develop their own unique voices. And that may be true, in part. On the other hand, like most serious artists, we wanted to materialize, to be heard and acknowledged as authentic by outside recognition. We needed a readership.

What were young women poets to do, understanding clearly by then the rules of the game and how we must submit our language to the scrutiny of those in power? What if we carried in us the seeds of a rebellion that didn't want to follow the leader? What if we wanted to write, unhampered by group worship of whatever aesthetic theory was in current vogue; to cross boundaries and give voice to impurities involving shifting grounds of feeling and intellect? We were learning and selecting what we could from each encountered poet and teacher. But there was something more, glowing in the dark. We didn't know what to name it yet, but some of us wanted to locate a poetics on our own terms. We had always been the marginalized sex, looking toward the center, and from our point-of-view there was reporting yet to be done.

For me, the awakening began out of some combination of Simone de Beauvoir's call to consciousness in *The Second Sex,* Adrienne Rich's grave and alarming poem "The Roofwalker," and Barbara Guest's tenacious insistence on the primacy of reinventing language structures in order to catch one's own at-oddness with the presumed superiority of the central mainstream vision. Quietly at first, then very actively, variations of this perception began to surface. The women's movement came on strong, and poetry was at the center of it. Finally, one imagined, there would be a warm room where the multiple styles of women's minds and bodies and poetic languages could flower.

But, in fact, something else happened. There were political needs—raw, bottled-up feelings wanting out—and a call for the immediately accessible language of personal experience as a binding voice of women's strength. Many women focused on the poem as a place for self-expression, for giving a true account, for venting rage, and for embracing sexual love of women. The lesbian political vision became particularly potent and powerful in writing; the suddenly perceived freedom of women to claim their power through their love and support of one another could no longer be denied. So powerful were their voices that a new center evolved in the Seventies, a poetics organized and dominated by the aesthetic vision of women-centered literary magazines such as *Sinister Wisdom, 13th Moon,* and *Conditions*—often lesbian and separatist in ideology and almost exclusively focused on poems of content that described and reinforced the values and life-styles shared by this community.

It was in the early stages of this forming center that I came to San Francisco, an emerging yet vocally timid feminist, to direct the Poetry Center and to teach at San Francisco State. These were probably the most isolated years of my writing life. I knew many poets but, although I enjoyed some as social friends, I had no true community. I no longer wanted to "submit" work to abstract male editors and try calmly to absorb their well-meaning but mostly patronizing "corrections" of my work. And yet it seemed clear to me that neither my way of working nor my sexual orientation would be deemed appropriate for these lesbian/feminist journals.

In that necessary but painful phase of feminism in the Seventies, heterosexual women were often regarded as politically untrustworthy, despite their intense friendships with women and their activism on behalf of the women's community. Also, there was the very real problem of one's interest in non-traditional poetic works. I'd long since been compelled by the linguistic inventions of Gertrude Stein and by Virginia Woolf's complex interior monologues—the resistance and playfulness of dictions peculiarly odd, peculiarly at odds with standard "accessible" modes of expression in poems and prose works. I recognized a structural order of fragmentation and a linguistic resistance to law-abiding traditional models that confirmed my perspective. I wanted this difference in my own work. Yet, ironically, this fascination with the innovative works of modernist women writers marginalized me even further from the official women's writing community. I continued to write, but I very seldom sent out work to journals.

Eventually, I got to know several Bay Area poets whose work and thought became increasingly important to me. Their focus brought me to a different kind of attentiveness: it wasn't the witty polish or posturing of "great lines," but a listening attitude, an attending to unconscious connections, a backing-off of the performing ego to allow the mysteries and "mind" of language to come forward and resonate more fully. It was at this time that I began seriously reading H.D., Jack Spicer, and George Oppen. Theirs was quite a different attitude toward poetry than I'd absorbed in New York. I was stimulated to reach further into the silence of my own work.

I began to meet rather regularly with two women poets, Frances Jaffer and Beverly Dahlen, to read and criticize our own poetry and to discuss our growing involvement with feminist practice and how it converged with our writing. We shared our uncomfortable feelings of marginality vis-á-vis the women's writing community and our attraction to the various writings coming out of the modernist project. Our collective female experience of multiplicity and fragmentation and our wanting to locate that—structurally—in the look and sound of our poems seemed to find a sympathetic family tradition there, as well as support for our resistance to certain academic emphases with which we were not in tune.

We began to talk increasingly about whether there might be a difference between female and male perception, located in the poetic language men and women chose to express their experience. Not that the three of us wrote alike, but it did appear that there were certain gender-oriented preoccupations and distinctions we shared. Our aesthetic and political concerns began making increasingly rigorous demands upon us, causing us each to become more intellectually exacting and artistically inventive in our writing. Without each other's support at that time, none of us would have written as much or as well. But the more we wrote, the less we fit into anything. In our shared ideology and our poetic practice, we were not pure: neither purely, categorically avant-garde nor purely one kind of feminist, Marxist, Freudian, or Lacanian. All these directions had their variant pull in us and stimulated work.

But the question remained—where could we publish our work? Who might be interested in what we were doing? Sometimes a few wishful fantasies of making our own journal surfaced, but no one could quite imagine adding that labor to already demanding work schedules. Then a year or so went by without our meeting as a group; we each had things to sort out in our own lives and writing. In a certain sense we were treading water when it came to our continually voiced unhappiness at the lack of a definable audience. We parted as a writing group, without parting as friends, in an unresolved drift toward privacy that felt both necessary and frustrating. I went to Europe for six months, and getting away gave me distance and time to think. All our conversations echoed in my mind. Our isolation as writers was a dilemma I could neither let go of nor find a solution for.

When I got back in the fall of 1981, I was scheduled to teach a course called "Feminist Poetics," which I'd introduced into the Creative Writing curriculum at San Francisco State University in order to consider—*within* the community of a classroom—the very questions that had been pressing upon me for years. Why was there no specifically acknowledged tradition of modernist women's poetry continuing out of H.D., Stein, Dorothy Richardson, Woolf, Mina Loy, Djuna Barnes, Laura Riding, Lorine Niedecker, and Marianne Moore as there clearly was for men working out of the Pound-Williams-Olson tradition or the Stevens-Auden lineage? Why had most of the great women modernists been dropped cold from reading lists, anthologies and university curricula? And why were most feminist and traditional critics failing to develop any interest in contemporary women poets working to bring structural and syntactic innovation into current poetic practice?

Then there were also the puzzling questions of language and gender, which were being argued convincingly, often from opposite positions. Did female experience require a totally different language, as Luce Irigaray seemed to suggest? How was that difference located in usage, a usage that had perhaps occurred and been ignored, dismissed as insignificant, or dropped out of the canon and quickly absorbed—at times, actively appropriated—by powerful male figures in the writing community? How was gender expressed and imprinted socially?

Teaching this class raised my distress level as it simultaneously gave me strength of purpose. Something more had to be done. There was a conversation with my writer-friend, Bob Glück, that sticks in my mind. It began with the above symptoms of distress and finished, for me, with his gentle but clear statement: "Kathleen, you must decide who your audience is and then address it." He was not talking about the private act of writing.

I went away again for the summer with that sentence dogging me, and my resolve became clear. I began formulating a tentative plan for a modest-size journal, which I hoped to lure my writing-group colleagues into being part of. I missed our particular way of talking and the feeling of support that came from it. There was no longer any question in my mind. I had to give time to making a place where our issues could be aired and some new choices put forward in women's poetry—asserted and selected by women—including a revival of modernist figures and a closer look at contemporary work discounted by critics. I wanted a serious yet *in*formal conversation among poets and scholar/teacher/critics.

I wrote to my scholar friend, Annette Kolodny, and asked her if such a project seemed of use to her. I wanted to know if she thought it would be taken seriously by the feminist critical community, whose books we poets were reading but whom we imagined as a fairly insular group with minimal interest in what were, for us, burning issues. I suggested to her that perhaps women critics simply didn't know how to begin thinking or talking about the more innovative compositional work going on and the seriousness of its quest. Perhaps there was some fear?

I wondered if it would be of help to scholars if each poet were asked to write "Working Notes" about her particular writing process. It might also be useful for the poets—as well as the formally trained scholar-critics—to do informal commentary on books by other women. Perhaps new insights and descriptions coming directly from the poets might provide useful clues for the careful detective work in which scholar-critics engaged?

Annette agreed with all these speculations and assured me that she would welcome such an attempt. Her letter was the final encouragement I needed. I returned to San Francisco and talked with Frances and Bev, who both agreed to give it a try. I suggested that we enlist, as contributing editors, two feminist scholars whose essays we'd been reading and discussing in our writing group and who had become friends in the process: Carolyn Burke and Rachel Blau DuPlessis. Two years into our venture, when Beverly could no longer continue as an active editor, a poet-scholar, Susan Gevirtz took her place, adding new perspective to our enterprise.

That's the gestation part. But to show what a collective labor it was to name our journal, let me share my notes on our first meeting, in which we were searching for a name that would identify us clearly. The ideas came flying fast, as in a jazz improvisation of three instruments, where one voice comments on the phrase played by another, a movement of call and response, until some new resolution of the classic tune has been achieved. The suggestions started with *Parts of Speech,* then *Feminine Endings* (after Judy Grahn's poem), then *Indefinite Article,* then *Text/ure, Alice Blue Gown, Red Tulips,* and *Para/phrase.* Next came *Where (we) are,* then *I (too)* — as in Marianne Moore's line about poetry: "I, too, dislike it" — and, finally, *HOW(ever)* from her next line; "However, there is a place for it."

First, *However* was one word; then we broke it into its typographical and parenthetical components. The name represented for us an addendum, a point-of-view from the margins, meant to flesh out what had thus far been proposed in poetry and poetics.

There were problems in asserting a point-of-view that defined itself as female and often feminist, and in making a magazine devoted solely to the publication of women writers. Some people inevitably felt excluded, as seems to happen whenever a new aesthetic is asserted publicly. Given the territorial bias we've all been subjected to in Western culture, the expectation of exclusion seems to be almost automatically programmed. But rather than seeing ourselves as exclusionary or here to displace or replace anything or anyone, we hoped instead to be an added source of information and stimulation. One thinks of Dada, Surrealism, Futurism, Black Mountain, the Harlem Renaissance, the New York School and recent Language-centered propositions and knows that there is plenty of room for exploration of multiplicity in poetry and theory being practiced by women, without destroying our basic support of one another. The reward for asserting a vision is to become visible, to participate actively in the wider literary conversation, and to help in creating a community that has been waiting to come into view. It turns out, in our case, that there had been many women like us, feeling isolated for years — excluded from the aesthetic or political mandates of existing poetics.

But there is another question raised by Johanna Drucker in a talk at the Cannessa Park Gallery in San Francisco and, in a different way, by Nina Auerbach in her paper, "Engorging the Patriarchy," delivered at the Cal Tech conference on "Marxism and Feminism." Both Auerbach and Drucker have addressed the potentially dangerous position into which women writers may put themselves by continuing to see themselves as marginal—either in their use of language or in specific, characteristic styles of living, writing, or thinking. Both fear that in attempting to explore or even define a new terrain, we may be cutting ourselves off from access to the patriarchy (or, in our case, the matriarchy as well)—the existing power lines and energy sources clearly necessary to our survival. Drucker suggests that we ought no longer to identify our differences, but should merge with "the genderless project of literature" and take our places confidently, rather than spend more time writing a scenario of difference and marginality.

Auerbach sees that "feminist ideology is inseparable from the lived knowledge of subordination, just as reading and writing are part of our continual self-authorization and self-authentication." She wants us to enter into the discourse, so as to deflate the phantasmic powers we have projected onto our subordinators and begin to see them more in scale as flawed individuals asserting their ideas. But she warns that any form of discourse perceived, even if not intended, as separatist is always a double-edged sword: the very qualities that women are praised for having, then risk becoming an institutionalized enterprise, rigidly enforced and prohibiting the edge of difference from continuing to find its ever-changing voice. She is afraid that if we make too absolute a definition of the uniformity and uniqueness of women's writing, we will be quickly embraced and as quickly absorbed and effaced by well-meaning critics, only to disappear with Zelda Fitzgerald and Dorothy Wordsworth into the footnotes of self-proclaimed male truths. As she suggests:

> Our stress on our uniformity and uniqueness in culture may make us look frailer and more boring than we are. . . . Our own complicity in this isolation may invite scholars to define us in reductive formulas they do not apply to more intimately known material. . . . [It] may make us . . . appear too special for the gross machinery of scholarship. (Auerbach 1987, 152)

While I take seriously these voiced fears, they arrive at a time when we are experiencing a new inner strength and integration from activity we see not as separatist but, more accurately, as shedding light upon a burgeoning group of women poets—poets who are unique, though quite definitely *not* uniform, and who have consistently been neglected by academic, mainstream, feminist, and avant-garde scholar/critics. Instead of waiting to be approved by this or that established authority (or invited into the dance by an imagined mentor), we've engaged in urgent sifting and digging, meaning to reconstruct that pre-existing tradition of modernist women who need us to acknowledge them as much as we need them to fall back on for daring and spiritual renewal, so that we may set out a light for whatever next unknown voices are laboring in the dark.

It is from this assertion of a point-of-view, through the editing of *HOW*(*ever*), that I began to demystify for myself the forms of power, the totems and secret caves of taste-making in the literary world. It is precisely in proposing a poetics of sufficient depth and complexity to satisfy our own hungers—as well as participating in the "dig" for a female tradition of linguistic invention—that we begin to starve the larger-than-life figures who have dominated and denied us. Not only do we exorcise their neglect, but we understand the commitment and hard work they have brought to the literatures they've found valuable. Thus, from that edge or brink or borderline we call the margin, we are able to create another center . . . a laboratory in which to look for the unknown elements we suspect are there.

How did Emma Slide?
A matter of gestation

In the early 1970s, I was living through a pattern that turned out to be somewhat classic among American women of my age: the break-up of a first marriage (entered into during the role-dominated Sixties), and the struggle to function simultaneously as working mother living alone with child, artist trying to pursue her writing, and passionate creature wanting love yet unhappy with the forms that had been thus far provided for it in our culture. For endless months the struggle raged internally, with a state of celibacy often providing the necessary cocoon for survival of the new self trying to evolve slowly toward an unfamiliar yet authentic way of being.

At that time, writing about the needs and doubts and paranoid suspicions around romantic love—its old doxology of sexual images and expectations confined by the very structure of love-language as we knew it—proved to be an enormously awkward and inhibiting task. It immediately plunged one into feelings of embarrassment and exposure. After all, society's frame for the ideal relationship was as impeccable and beyond

FRAME: This narrative was generated by a women's writing conference held at University of California–Santa Cruz, in the summer of 1978, attended by (among others) Maggie Anderson and Mary Margaret Sloan, both of whom subsequently urged me to write up my podium-improvised term: "the gestate." It was later printed in Anderson's journal *Trellis* 3 (1979), and in a revised version, in *Feminist Poetics: A Consideration of the Female Construction of Language*, edited by Kathleen Fraser and Judy Frankel (San Francisco, Calif.: University Printing Services, San Francisco State University, 1984).

question as a well-cut silk dress—a little swish to the skirt, but no threads hanging from the hem.

But in the Seventies, nothing was certain. One edged up to a feeling and withdrew two days later. Fully developed systems, balanced syllogisms, neat packages of future life appeared to be contrary to one's experience. And then there was all that anger, seeing one's anxiously held hopes dissolve: if you tried to give this anger voice in the poem, it risked at any moment becoming overburdened with its own conviction to the point of cliché. How, then, to express out-of-control experience within the controls offered thusfar in our literary dowry?

At the end of 1973, being of stalwart heart and shriveled libido, my life and writing began to tire of struggling in isolation; the safety of containment no longer seemed to dominate as an instinct. Rather, there was a hunger to move out again into the dangerous but dynamic world, a willingness to take chances, once more, with the heart. Within the same month, two phenomena presented themselves to me. The first was a name, Emma Slide, which dropped into my mind one day as I was vacuuming. I was intrigued by that name since I'd never known anyone named Emma and had no immediate associations with it. My poet-taster's love of pure word texture directed me to write it down. Just that.

The second event was the appearance of a very interesting person in my life, who was as ready and wanting to fall in love as I was. Our geographical distance—three thousand miles between coasts—only fed the initial set of images provided by a brief meeting in New York, and we proceeded, through the fiction of letters, to develop a scenario in which we were the two romantic leads. By the time he came to visit me in California, the old romantic clichés I'd been trying so hard to wean from my psychological lexicon were already at work, pre-shaping our experience, heightening our expectations, programming us toward certain conversations and core romantic interludes replete with the expected set of props—fine wine, seaside hide-away, full moon.

These prefatory autobiographical remarks seem important to the discussion I wish to develop, for they set out the dilemma that I subsequently chose to write about through the character (magically given me) of Emma

Slide. The writing, in fact, became my touchstone, my tool for keeping in contact with the disparity between that which my former "self" still wished for and that which, in fact, was really being experienced by the newer, less certain self-in-progress.

Just before my friend from the East came to visit, I'd gone to the stationer's to buy an address book and had spied a beautiful little black ledger, bound in red leather with gold lettering. I decided to buy it for no reason other than my attraction to its proportions and colors and, no doubt, its suggestion of order. When I got home and began looking at the ledger, I wrote "The Story of Emma Slide" in the front of it, again with no plan beyond that gesture. But it was a first move, setting in motion a process in my unconscious, alerting it toward a particular investigation and focus. Enter, New Year's Eve and the arrival of my friend—here (I thought) for a weekend business trip, here (he thought) to stay as long as was necessary to convince me of our future as a couple.

We were, as fate would have it, sharing a flat in which I'd knocked out all the walls in order to have more free-flowing light and space in my domestic life. Thus, there was an intimacy enforced by lack of private rooms and doors behind which one might retreat, assimilate, and remind oneself of the larger picture. The ledger, at that point, suddenly became a survival handbook. It was the place I could retreat to in privacy and could make notations when outer events began to swamp me. I saw rather quickly that the ledger itself would help to determine the form of my writing—this non-poem that, nevertheless, was full of images, lyric bursts, carefully observed details in the natural world we two were inhabiting. I took on the persona of Emma Slide like a costume or mask that expressed some very real part of me—some voice that had been too small and baffled to risk its nakedness as *my* voice in my "regular" poems.

As well as adapting the journal-entry or day-book idea in this ledger, I also tapped into the word "ledger" and its function as a place in which one made an accounting of debits and credits, of resources spent and earned. And I applied that function metaphorically to the emotional expenditures I wanted to account for in this log, written during the progress of our romantic interlude. It gave me space to move around in, to unload annoyances, romantic illusions caught mid-flight; it invited me into a sense of the absurd, particularly vis à vis my "self," caught up in the net of my own weaving.

It was a form of writing that didn't bully me into the traditional beginning, middle, and end — the linear model of organizing a poem that had so largely comprised my university-educated ideas about writing poetry. It gave me a chance to unfold the movements attributed to right-brain perception — intuitive leaps, simultaneous and related paths of taking in information and, at the same time, to make fun of the didactic and self-conscious defining of this phenomenon in myself. In this fragmented form of notation, I didn't have to carry around the authoritarian shadow on my shoulders, conserving its left-margin narrative preference. What was happening was not logical, nor could it be understood accurately in a forwardly progressing model. There were, in fact, many stops and starts, pauses and rewinds . . . and frames of silence.

The writing wanted to reflect what was turning out to be a painful breaking-down process, a pageant set out in scenes depicting each of my romantic illusions and why they would no longer hold up, given the consciousness I'd worked so hard for and could not now turn my back on (even though the "old me" wished to). These scenes were neither neatly played out nor carefully staged as, say, an eight-part poem (of fourteen lines each) might demonstrate. Instead, they were full of small undramatic exchanges and insights, as in the second entry, when an interior monologue begins trying to deal with the obvious discrepancy between the romantic ideal and the reality Emma perceives in herself and her new lover. This entry gives Emma a place within the "poem" to retreat, to back off from immediate pressures and to listen to what the infant-now-adolescent self is trying to assert and, in that acknowledgment, to gain as territory for the future. Thus, Emma questions:

> Is this what she wants? A repetitive nature.
> No, but to grow plant-like
> from the center
> but new.
>
> (Fraser 1974, 44)

The theme of interruption has often been alluded to in describing the character of the daily lives of women whose role as nurturer in the home and the larger societal arena is largely taken for granted, depriving them of the long periods of silence and solitude normally associated with creative production. Emma's slow burn begins to heat up (in the third and fourth entries) as she perceives how much rage she feels at being constantly intruded upon and at the enormous need for privacy that has gathered and grown monstrous inside her by its very denial on the part of her lover (and earlier, her child), who cannot seem to carry out an action or experience a thought without falling into this habit of dependency upon her—the mother—for a response, an encouraging stroke, or a punishing denial of herself.

In revealing this resentment, Emma is taking chances. But writing fictionally—within her persona—acknowledging that she was only one of many voices in me, made it possible to admit to feelings and perceptions normally reserved for a private journal. A formal device was thus discovered for detailing information—intimate, yet political to its very roots. An old idea, to be sure, spoken through theatrical and fictional characters, but now adapted and collaged with poetic structures of rhythm and line and distillation to form a new way of moving in the poem, a way that discovered itself out of necessity.

.

In the summer of 1977, I was talking with a group of women writers who had gathered for a two-week summer retreat at the University of California at Santa Cruz to focus on their own work and to enter into dialogue on female forms in writing. As we were waiting one afternoon for the door to be unlocked to the room where I was scheduled to read, a woman in her thirties said to me somewhat matter-of-factly: "I'm putting off my writing until my kids are grown up." The statement left me angry and speechless for the moment. I realized the reality and difficulty her statement was coming from, but I also knew that she had experienced acquiescence on the part of her friends on other occasions when she'd defined the pattern of her future.

My mind was working double-time. I was thinking about childbirth, its interior unfolding process; then child-rearing and the infinite interruptions it promises. How we want them, how we don't . . . that the ambivalence for women artists around the issue of children and mates will never be resolved. I thought of the word "gestation" in this context, and when I stood up to read, I began, first, to speak of our survival-as-artist needs and suggested that it was time we formally acknowledged this interruptive pattern as an exact set of movements, a newly evolved poem model that carried its own imprint from the recognized and partly intentional nature of our lives. I named this new form the *Gestate* and defined it thus:

> The *Gestate* is a poetic form of unnumbered discrete phrases, unfolding and proliferating as rapidly or as slowly as one's perceptions do. It takes as its reference the term, "gestation" and acknowledges—in this biological/intellectual carrying—all the uneven physical and emotional growth curves that express themselves, recognizing the value of precise detail and the use of formal devices, while welcoming those unexpected and mysterious and necessary leaps in perception.

Although composed with a slightly tongue-in-cheek regard for the high seriousness we wordsmiths love to apply to theory, this definition still remains useful as a way of regarding fragmented experience and shifting points-of-view as a legitimate grid over which such souls as Emma can attempt their journey.

The way ideas are juxtaposed to form a text says more about the intentions of the writer than the content

When I lived on Liberty Street (late Sixties), in my first San Francisco dwelling, there was a house situated behind and just up the slope of the hill from mine. Near the front steps of this house was a flagpole that I had a clear view of from my back window, near the kitchen where I spent a good deal of time preparing food for my child, David, then only a year old.

Between domestic tasks, I would use the kitchen table as my writing desk. There was a period of some six months at this "writing-desk" in which I would randomly look uphill in the direction of the flagpole and see brightly colored flags flying. Often in the space of a day there would be several different flags waving simultaneously from the pole, or the first flag (seen in the morning) would change in the afternoon. I liked the red, blue, and green diagonals and the occasional half-moon or star. I was pleasured and mystified by the flags and made up many stories to explain their existence. Never once did I see the tenant of the house go out to raise or lower his flags, yet I was very much in touch with his imagination, stimulated to a possible code of events I might someday crack. Flags began appearing in my poems. I eventually found a book illustrating the International Code of Signals, a visual code system devised for use by ships at sea.

·

FRAME: This piece was written as a talk for a series of panels initiated in 1983 by Small Press Traffic, this one put together by the prose writer Michael Amneson. My title is from Amneson's working title for the panel. It was the first time I dealt head-on with the anxiety of public discourse.

The first International Code was drafted in 1855 by a committee
set up by the British Board of Trade. Flags at that time numbered
18, which represented the consonants of the alphabet, with the
exception of x and z. A later version published in 1899 increased
the letter flags to 26, plus an answering pennant. Flags, one for
each letter of the alphabet, are hoisted on the mast, singly or in
groups of two, three, four. Single and two flag hoists are distress
signals, three flag hoists are general signals, four flag hoists geographical signals. In addition, each flag has a name; A, Alpha, B,
Bravo, C, Charlie, etc. In combination, as CJD, "I was plundered by
a pirate," these signals constitute a complete volume of code signals. (Weiner 1982, Introduction)

•

The man who owned the flags did not know I was there at my window
receiving. I never found the occasion to tell him I'd been noticing. I felt
too shy, and my own life seemed so different from his. We spoke different
languages, as far as I could tell. From his point-of-view, he probably thought
I was simply a young mother with an infant, living a somewhat enclosed
and predictable life. At least that was the point-of-view I invented for him,
which meant that I projected my own limited view of myself onto his
facade and denied him receivership. I canceled out his further liveliness in
my life by deciding ahead of time what he thought about me. I did not
send to him, so he could not receive me. It is probably true that for him
there was the initial pleasure of combining those flags and hoisting them
up. But did *anyone* ever tell him they got the message?

•

One is reminded of Viktor Shklovshy's famed definition of art as
defamiliarization, especially the idea that "An image is not a permanent referent for those mutable complexities of life which are
revealed through it; its purpose is not to make us perceive meaning,
but to create a special perception of the object." (Perloff 1981, 115)

•

journal entry, Sept. 14
Michael Amneson is organizing a writers-on-writing panel and has asked
me and Steve Benson to participate. An additional, as yet unspecified, fourth

person will join us. In spite of my wariness of public speaking and even though I've declined other invitations to do so, I sense a shift in myself from anxiety to curiosity.

I check it out. What's messing-up my tidy defense system, about to leave me open for attack? I discover that it's the tug of these two persons, these bodies of writing. Furthermore, I am intrigued by Michael's social gesture. Even though he appears to be shy, he is consciously asserting his presence, represented by his point-of-view on the occasion of this gathering that he has initiated. What is equally interesting is that he's asking other writers to help him. He's not letting his shyness prevent him from making a statement, nor is he pretending to be an isolated individual who has no need of community — someone who can sustain a writing life in a vacuum of pride.

•

Alienation forces withdrawal into the self. The alienated person is thrown on his own resources because he finds none offered him by society. In self-defense, he is driven to imagine himself as a self-sufficient, self-contained atom of existence. This emphasis on the rugged, independent self lends the contract theory of society a specious plausibility because it leads *us,* the alienated, to believe we are fully realized persons prior to the creation (and re-creation) of society and to ignore society's role in the creation of persons. Unified, realized persons and unified, realized societies come into existence simultaneously. (Bierman 1973, 50–51)

•

journal entry, Sept. 15

I was first drawn to Steve's work when I heard him read publicly and saw him enact, via his continuously repositioned body, the situation of uncertainty. He shared the baffled seriousness of brilliant clowns such as Stan Laurel. Since then, we've exchanged work and many conversations. He brings out my playfulness, I bring out his arguments. I admire Steve as a unique force in the writing community because of his inventive performances. He activates a climate of risk, between himself and his audience, often improvising on the written text, in the very moment of performance. At this edge of uncertainty, he at once makes himself extremely vulnerable and puts his audience in touch with its own shifting identities and tentatively held positions. Listening to him, I lighten up. Immense reserves of withholding are released. I find myself laughing at myself, in him.

I am grateful, as well, for the work Steve does within the writing community. It is time-consuming and often difficult to write a review of another person's book, to direct or write or act in a play. On the other hand, it appears to give him pleasure to make this effort. I like the idea of participating with Steve in the risky community dialogue that he enjoys; also, I want to give him something in return for the ideas and sheer energy he has shared with me privately and publicly over the years. Is desire replacing the habit of wariness? Perhaps an exchange can take place.

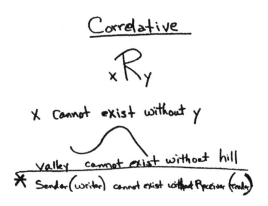

Fig 1. A correlative

A correlative is something—for example, a buyer—that stands in some relation to something else—for example, a seller. . . . Something that is a buyer is a correlative; it is a correlative to a seller. A parent and child are correlatives. Correlatives are tied with bonds of necessity. There cannot be a parent unless there is a child; and vice versa. (Bierman 1973, 72)

Steve and Michael are both individual selves and social beings. They are correlatives, in that they are senders or writers. A "sender" cannot exist without a "receiver." A writer has trouble existing for long without a reader. When I read Michael's words or listen to Steve perform, I am the receiver to their sender and in this way we help to make each other's existence as writers possible. But what about the sender part of me, sitting in shy isolation at my kitchen table? How can I have an existence as a writer if I do not have a receiving audience? How can I hope for a receiver to complete my existence if I am unwilling to take the risk of being a sender?

•

journal entry, Sept. 19

The panel is to be called "The way ideas are juxtaposed to form a text says *more* about the intentions of the writer than the content." Thinking about this, I'm slightly uncomfortable. I discover that it is the word "more" to which I object. I'd like to suggest the substitution of something that would describe a distinction rather than reinforcing a hierarchical relation. "More" seems to suggest "better."

Meanwhile, the old panic sets in. If I put myself in front of an audience that may include those whom I've characterized in the past as authoritarian or judgmental, then I'm choosing a situation in which very little of what I really care about can be revealed because most of my emotional focus will be defensive, trying to protect myself from being canceled out by what I project as my critic's frozen view of me. The thoughts I once discovered as relevant may disintegrate into babble.

[Worst-case scenario: My memory suddenly jams. Single words disappear and what they were directed toward changes from solid to liquid to steam. I stand dumbstruck, without voice.]

•

The condition of affliction—as described by Simone Weil— is the primary condition of the powerless. This condition is characterized above all by speechlessness.

It is important to realize the alliance of speechlessness and powerlessness; that the former maintains the latter; that the powerful are dedicated to the investiture of speechlessness on the powerless.

Speechlessness—as I have known/know it—is implosive, not ex-

plosive. . . . Speechlessness begins with the inability to speak; this
soon develops into the inability to act. The inability to act is part
of the implosion.

(Cliff 1984, 103)

·

journal entry, Oct. 1

I thought of a fourth member for the panel and have suggested Gail
Sher. Her poems are constructed in a way that illustrates and maps her
own interior linguistic perspective on the world, the unique way in which
she hears and places words as part of her thought process. Gail has a self-
containment yet an availability that puts me at ease. I'm actually beginning
to think about the panel with anticipation.

·

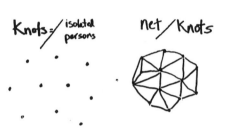

Fig 2. Net knots

·

Perhaps another image might help you to grasp the concept of a
person that I am advocating. Picture a net. Let the net represent a
society, the net knots — not the string of the knots — represent
persons, and the string between the net knots represent relations.
If we were to cut the strings that lead from a net knot to other net
knots, what *was* a net knot would become a detached, knotted
string but it would no longer be a net knot. If you cut all a body's
relations to other bodies, you have made relating impossible for it.
. . . If someone pulls on a given knot, it will effect the other knots

in the net. What is done to you or by you is done to others in your society. (Bierman 1973, 78–79)

·

journal entry, Nov. 19

Michael just called to say that Gail has canceled. She is working on a "bread book" and her deadline is putting so much pressure on her that she will not have time to think about her talk for the panel. He feels baffled by this but has accepted her withdrawal. I feel disappointed, cheated of Gail's potential presence and support as another poet whose sensibility I'm very much in touch with, partly because she is a woman with a shared perspective and partly because I've been working on a critical piece about her new book of poems and feel particularly connected, at this moment, to her language.

My fantasy is that Gail has baked bread many times and knows what needs to be said about it . . . but she has not been on *this* kind of panel before and has no model, even though there are a number of words/thoughts moving around in her head. Perhaps she is missing an organizing principle for her talk or a source of physical expansion such as yeast might provide for bread dough. I feel I cannot do my part as well if she's not there, so I must try to think of some way of convincing her to reconsider. Maybe she could just read bread recipes juxtaposed with quotes from Gertrude Stein as commentary. I decide to telephone her.

·

journal entry, Nov. 20

. . . that we are limited by others' descriptions of how our life is, or should appear to be . . . until the feeling of entrapment becomes so claustrophobic that we have to make an opening and let the inner life, which feels closer, truer, come forth into written language on the page where it is palpable—but safe and unexposed . . . and silent (unless read aloud).

What we want to say may seem too blatant because of crossing boundaries of protocol, such as the appropriate way to present a talk on a panel. How we learn to pull back, keep within the terms agreed upon—a tolerable, mediated volume.

Perhaps if I recorded my voice on tape, I could be sure of what was there, revealing itself. The tape recorder would be next to me and in control. If I didn't stutter or forget, while reading a patch of material onto a tape while in a room alone then perhaps, if sitting at a table in front of a group of people, I could maintain eye-contact.

                                        .

(Later . . .) I just called Gail and suggested that anything *could* be interesting, and that she should try not to let her fears of not being "perfect," according to others' standards, imperil her own chance to contribute to the community conversation. I mentioned that I'd announced her appearance to the members of my Poetics seminar, that they were anticipating her in-person presentation. I could feel her begin to change her mind. She really wanted to participate but needed support. She suddenly agreed to do it, and I felt my anticipation return. It's clear that some other self sits to one side, ready to change his or her mind at any moment. Knowing this dialectical shift in myself, I feel reassured.

Perhaps in maintaining my habit of regarding audience authority warily, I've devised a convenient holding action—a way of preventing myself from having to engage with the difficult anxiety (or challenge) of actively contributing my uncertain point-of-view. I recognize the truth of this, not as in a mirror but more like an unexpected glance in a plate glass window when you've caught yourself frowning in deep concentration, thinking all the while you were walking along like a neutral person.

The Blank Page: H.D.'s invitation to trust and mistrust language

> we know no rule
> of procedure,
>
> we are voyagers, discoverers,
> of the notknown
>
> the unrecorded;
> we have no map . . .
>
> —H.D., "The Walls Do Not Fall," *Trilogy*

With an authentic sense of beginning at Zero, a poetically mature H.D. could write in the war years of the early 1940s: "we know no rule / of procedure." Yet her contemporary readers know that rules of procedure did exist at almost every level of her early life. Even in that nontraditional world of literature she leaned toward, achieved forms stood in place. Nevertheless, she refused the finality of the already filled page. For while others' writings often thrilled her, they did not speak for the unsaid that burned in her.

Born from doubt and extreme privacy, her own tentative language slowly invented itself out of silence. Her gift was an ability to see the empty page waiting to be inscribed and to imagine — beyond the parchment metaphor of "palimpsest" — a contemporary model for the poem that would recover a complex overlay of erotic and spiritual valuings variously imprinted,

---

FRAME: This essay was originally written as a talk, at the invitation of Donna Hollenberg, who chaired the H.D. panel at the American Literature Association meetings in May 1997 in San Diego. She asked me to look at my writing practice in relationship to the work of H.D. and to speculate on any influence. Later Hollenberg developed that idea with a number of other American women poets into a collection of essays to be called *H.D. and Poets After*, forthcoming in 1999 from the University of Iowa Press.

then worn away . . . then, finally, re-discovered and engraved inside her own lines. Her vision lay in the conviction of plurality—that the blank page would never be a full text until women writers (and their reader-scholars) scrawled their own scripts across its emptiness.

Even within Pound's mentoring embrace, H.D. felt a certain cautionary guardedness around the unfolding, if uneasy, project of her own work. "Ezra would have destroyed me and the center they call 'Air and Crystal,'" she admits in 1958 in her journal entry from *End to Torment*. A month later, she writes: "To recall Ezra is to recall my father. . . . To recall my father is to recall the cold blazing intelligence of my 'last attachment' of the war years in London. This is not easy" (from H.D.'s journal entries for April 9 and May 15, 1958).

She had survived two major wars and the tyranny of gender stereotype. But fifty years later she was still trying to sort out the impact of this strange, impassioned outsider, Ezra Pound, who identified and constellated her early poetic identity while at the same time limiting its very stretch by his defining, instructive approval.

That a strong push-pull dynamic progressively marks her writer-relation to Pound and her position "on the fringes of the modernist main-stream" seems evident from passages in her fictional works and in bits of letters and journals (Friedman and DuPlessis 1981). Her artistic progress is marked by self-initiated shifts in attitude and ambition—notably, her decision to try to shed the once-useful but finally limiting description of "Imagiste" given her by Pound as her poet designator. It is instructive to mark her ambivalence toward—and discomfort with—male value judgements vis à vis her own work and to see how she climbed, repeatedly, out of these silencing effects to again recover her own voice and to trust its foraging instincts.

We read the following words written to Pound, anticipating his criticism, in a note H.D. sent along to him in 1959 with a copy of her complete *Helen in Egypt:* "Don't worry or hurry with the Helen—don't read it at all—don't read it yet—don't bother to write of it" (Friedman and DuPlessis 1981). One hears the echo and ricochet of her wariness traveling all the way back to Pound's first decisive claim on her poetic gifts, the swift and confident slash of his editor's pencil and his literal initialing—or label-

ing—of her for purposes of identification and value in the poetry market-
place.

In H.D.'s life, this style of "help" manifested itself in various powerful
guises, notably in encounters with big-affect literary friends such as D. H.
Lawrence, whose charismatic male authority was often as much a source
of anxiety as support. The delicate yet powerful mythic terrain wisely appropriated by H.D. afforded protection from a merely personal accounting
of her highly volatile emotional life—the more personal lyric, so liable to
deliver her into the hands of male "correction." Myth finally provided a
route of independent travel, a large enough page on which to incise and
thus emplace her own vision of the future, spiritually enlivened by values
retrieved from female life.

When she directs our attention in *Trilogy* to "the blank pages / of the
unwritten volume of the new" (103), H.D. is issuing a literal invitation of
breathtaking immensity and independence to contemporary women poets. Once perceived, the page is there and yours to re-make. No more
alibis. The challenge is at once freeing and awesome.

·

As a contemporary writer, I have been called back to this blank page
again and again. Let me attempt to describe a largely intuitive gathering-
up of poem materials for a serial work of mine, "Etruscan Pages" (Fraser
1993, 8–34; 1997, 97–118), in which the layerings of old and new inscriptions were built from accretions of literal archeological remnant bound
together into current pages of language, visual figure, and event (present-
time dreams and letters).

I believe that it was H.D.'s profound connection to the contemporary
relevance of ancient cultures—as well as her Egyptian experience with
hieroglyph as a kind of telegram from the atemporal—which opened me
and prepared me for my journey (May 1991) to the sites of three Etruscan
necropoli—Tarquinia, Vulci, and Norchia—scattered north of Rome along
the Maremma coast, each site marked on the map with an almost illegible
triangle of black dots. Having deferred a long-held intellectual curiosity,
early prompted by reading D. H. Lawrence in the Sixties and an early draft
(1979) of Rachel Blau DuPlessis's ground-breaking essay, "For the Etruscans"
(DuPlessis 1990, 1–19)—and thinly veneered with bookish obligation—I

finally took the occasion of a friend's visit to propose a journey to these three sites, and we set off early one morning with map and guidebook.

There was nothing that could have prepared me for the impact these places had on me—their absence informed by presence. The cliff tombs of Norchia might well have been entirely non-existent if one were dependent only upon visual clues or signs along nearby roads. By guesswork we found ourselves climbing down through rough rock passages overgrown with foliage that seemed to have been there forever. The lack of any other car or human allowed the presence of birds, local wild flowers, and the more apparent ruins of Roman conquerors—planted just across the ravine from the Etruscan cliff tombs—to resonate powerfully. I felt as if dropped through time, less and less able to talk casually of our surrounds.

Days later, the poem slowly began to rise to the surface of my listening mind. And during that time a startling convergence of dreams and events worked to push the limits of the poem into something much more layered and much less personal than any account of my own private experience could have provided. A week after the Maremma trip, I returned to the Villa Giulia, the major Etruscan museum in Rome, to see again the dancers lavishly flung across urns and the sculpted bodies of husband and wife entwined sensuously on the limestone lid covering an elongated sarcophagus. It was then I could finally begin to piece together their celebratory moment on earth with utterly changed eyes. H.D.'s invitation had allowed me to step out of the skin of verbal overlay and late-twentieth-century gloss, rendering me available to the palpable presence of these women and men.

Here are several passages from a letter, early embedded in my "page," that narrate a dream and then an archeological episode, both given to me during the weeks of the poem's writing . . . as if invented for the layered record I was attempting to rewrite:

> The night you left for Paros, I dreamt I was lying on a stone slab at the base of the cliff tombs at Norchia, preparing to make my transition from "this world" to "the other." I was thinking about how to negotiate the passage, when it came to me—the reason for all the layers of fine white cloth arranged and spread

around me. I said to you (because you were with me), "You just keep wrapping yourself with white cloth and eventually you are in the other place." (Fraser 1993, 26)

and this, from an unexpected conversation—days later—with an archeologist:

> The other source [referring to etymological studies] is the "mummy wrapping," linen originally from Egypt (probably hauled on trading ships) covered with formulaic and repetitious Etruscan religious precepts written "retro" (right to left). Even though there are over 1,200 words covering it, the total lexicon is barely 500. The mummy text is preserved in the museum in Zagreb, thus "The Zagreb Mummy." Her body had been wrapped in this shroud made of pieces of linen, written on through centuries [with Phoenician, Greek and, finally, Etruscan characters], used as "pages" for new writing whenever the old text had faded. Her family had wrapped her in this cloth, this writing, because it was available. (Fraser 1993, 27)

With these interventions, the actual making of the poem became immensely absorbing. H.D.'s exhortation to heed "the blank pages of the unwritten volume of the new" was pulling me away from her "air and crystal" language. My page wanted to be inscribed as if it were a canvas, my own linguistic motion and visual notation appropriating the Etruscan lexicon and alphabet as subject and object—inventions suggested directly from contact with tomb inscriptions and the beaten gold tablets at Villa Giulia, covered with the elusive remainders of their language.

For example, a passage on the imagined origins of the letter A is juxtaposed with a miniature lexicon composed of words that already existed throughout the larger poem's text, a word hand-scrawled in Etruscan letters (meant to resemble those scratched into burial stones) and a bit of quoted speculation by D.H. Lawrence. I wanted to place a close-up lens over particular words, as well as to foreground the hand and mind at work making language through history.

Without H.D.'s precedent, it is very unlikely that I would have trusted my own particular rendering of the historic clues and layers of the Etruscan culture, nor understood the urgency of articulating another reading of it in the face of all the officially recognized studies preceding me . . . including Lawrence's narrative. While my poem, "Etruscan Pages," intentionally acknowledges Lawrence's 1932 travel memoir, *Etruscan Places,* it writes the new word PAGE over the old word PLACE to tip the reader's attention in the direction of an optional reading introduced through a formal shift of perception. Mine is a document meant to record an alternative vision of the predominantly male archeological point-of-view already well-installed.

Having given Lawrence's account a rather perfunctory skim in the Sixties, I was curious to go back to it—once I had a fairly realized draft of my own—just to see what had occupied him. I was pleased but not that surprised to find that there were a number of physical details and baffling absences we'd noted in common—although sixty years apart—even to particulars of asphodel (he must have been there in May), and the "nothing" that seemed to be so present in the barren fields and shut tombs around Vulci where a sensuousness of daily life had once been so radiantly apparent.

I decided to incorporate several fragment phrases from Lawrence's text as a way of marking our meeting in parallel time—a kind of palimpsest dialogue. But I was deeply relieved to find that he'd not been to Norchia, the site that most profoundly spoke to me. I didn't want his brilliant voice-print preceding me everywhere. Its definite authority and well-installed literary history might have in some way inhibited me from capturing my own barely visible version.

·

I'd like to return now to the issue of asserted literary dominion versus self-confirmation, as it impinges on the working life of the woman poet. For in spite of her strategies for empowerment, we recognize in H.D.'s 1959 note to Pound a residual mistrust based on the tension between her deep desire for his approval and the necessary self-affirmation of her own unmediated—and thus uninhibited—vision and writing method. Even after fifty years, a lurking fear of not meeting his standards still seems to hover in her. It isn't a simple fear of critique, for she was obviously strong-willed and utterly conscious of her aesthetic choices by then; rather, it is more like the dread of having to tangle with the absolute ego of the beloved but intrusive father/judge, forever looming in the shadow just over her shoulder . . . and to risk the loss of his admiration.

·

Reviewing H.D.'s progress toward the trust of her own "page," a contemporary woman poet might well identify with this struggle to circumvent the tremendous pressure of prevailing male ideology that so conveniently persisted, historically viewing women contemporaries as "receptacle-like muses rather than active agents," thus reinforcing long-dominant "notions of what was properly and naturally feminine" (Friedman and DuPlessis 1981).

Recently reading through a selection of letters between Pound and the young Louis Zukofsky, exchanged between 1928 and 1930, I was generally amused until I came across such bits of Pound-heavy advice as his urging Zukofsky to form a new literary group of serious, high-energy writers but exhorting him: "NOT too many women, and if possible no wives at assembly. If some insist on accompanying their *mariti* [husbands], make sure they are bored and don't repeat offense. . . ." Later, advising Zukofsky about the selection of work for a new magazine, he says: "AND the verse used MUST be good . . . preferably by men [*sic*] under 30" (Pound and Zukofsky 1981).

In these tossed-off bits of pecking-order jocularity are found the not very subtle codes of selection and disenfranchisement that were practiced to various degrees in the literary world I entered as a young poet in the early Sixties. A primary difference between my world and H.D.'s was that nine-tenths of the once published writing by modernist women was out-of-print, leaving very few female texts as models for the nontraditional poetics one felt compelled to explore.

Fortunately, change was in the air. By the early Seventies, women scholars had begun to talk to each other about this problem and to investigate it in print.

·

This brings us again to the shaping hand of influence and the prevailing authority of installed standards of judgement . . . and how the effects of

gender-specific valuing, editing, and explication can make a radical difference in the continuing life of the working poet.

Thinking about particular writers who shaped my early writing sensibility, I cannot find any direct H.D. imprint upon my poetics or practice,
yet I know that somewhere along the line my mature writing has been
significantly touched by her traces even though in the first decade of my
exposure to modernist American poetry there was the now documented,
measurable obstacle blocking access to her writing.

I would guess that I first saw the initials *H.D.* at the end of an antholo-
gized poem sometime at the end of the Sixties. No doubt, that poem was
one of the few safe and untouchable Imagist poems that editors began
recirculating around that time to represent her work. We would later discover a much more complex, fecund, and demanding literary production.
But for the moment, lacking any particular professor's or admired poet's
passion for this mythic and (what seemed to me) very austere and impersonal voice, and swarmed as I was by every possible kind of innovative or
jazzy poetic example, I was not available to H.D.'s spiritual and generative
gift. I suspect that even if *Trilogy* or *Helen in Egypt* had been waved in my
face at this time, I lacked sufficient conscious appetite for her alchemical
and mythical vocabularies of transformation.

Eventually, in the mid-Eighties, I had the opportunity to read *Trilogy*
aloud with a small group of women poets and could finally hear H.D.'s
voice, as if there were no longer any barrier. By then, my inevitable share
of human loss had prepared me.

.

In the Sixties, I was in love with everything that promised a fresh start
and quite ready to shed a dominating mainstream "poetics of Self," impos-
ing its confessional hypnotic trance upon readers and young American
writers. I was chafing at the confines of the typical "I" centered, mainstream American poem that so theatrically and narcissistically positioned
the writer at the hub of all pain and glory; it seemed reminiscent of pre-
Renaissance science, before Galileo announced the radical news of his
telescopic discovery:

Man is no longer at the center of the universe

H.D. understood this afresh. The hierarchies forever asserting themselves were again toppled.

Physics, action painting, field poetics, and new music — as well as fuller readings of Woolf and new encounters with Richardson, Moore, and Stein, the New York school, the Black Mountain poets, and the Objectivists — had all been registering a different dynamic involving energy fields, shifting contexts, and a self no longer credibly unitary but divided and subdivided until uncertainty called into question any writing too satisfied with its own personal suffering or too narrowly focused on cleverness and polish.

My devotion and intellectual curiosity had been claimed instead by a dozen highly inventive, nontraditional sorts of poets. I imagined, then, that I was equally open to all poetry but, in fact, I was a young reader and writer, prone to the excitement of what I thought of as a high-modern tone and syntax, one whose surface diction and visual field promised to carry me away from what had begun to feel like the dangerous trap of lyric habit and ever closer to my own increasingly idiosyncratic compositions. I did not want to write within a language tradition too easily understood, too clearly part of an agenda rubber-stamped by most mainstream journals, but I had not yet articulated for myself the reasons for my resistance, nor the power relations dictating the limits of what I felt antagonistic toward.

The contemplative, as a desired place of knowledge, was beyond me; the contemporary implications and uses of myth hadn't yet hit — I mean, the understanding that myth is ahistoric, breathing in us and not merely confined to a narrative of the ancient past.

The Seventies and Eighties revealed a different grid, a detour meant to flaw the convenient, intact, uniform story of influence. As it turned out, H.D.'s linking of "hermetic" assignations with "secret language" and her conscious rejection of single-version narratives would become useful in helping to define my own poetic process. It was not that I wanted to write *like* her but, rather, that I began hearing her urgency and experiencing in her work a kind of female inspiriting guide that I'd been lacking.

·

Constructing and *re*constructing this episodic moment across the space of my own blank pages, I finally understood that H.D. had used the scaffolding of locked-up myth to regenerate lopsided human stories with a new infusion of contemporary perspective. This meant the possibility—for herself and her readers—of being more fully included in the ongoing pursuit of knowledge and thus less personally stuck in the isolation of private anguish. There was, as it turned out, a place in language—even in its zero beginnings—to put one's trust.

Partial local coherence
:
Regions with illustrations
(Some notes on "Language" writing)

L IN R

Why he wide by far wild thee
intimate or wadded say or Fold

that car's pet places,
afire, Stosh stood to fold

our wit stoves
green bill and border red

litt the old, slight young in falls'er
I d..

Lair met, strap, he reads
the pocket is & suit

bold board, fill through hair
what empties swell, it none

more no
no moment meant
yes meant, no.

—Tom Mandel, in the *Tuumba* postcard series
(Winter 1978)

"L IN R" is the first poem I remember seeing or responding to strongly that
was identified later as "language writing." The term had not become a part

---

FRAME: This piece was written in 1982 at the request of editor Michael Cuddihy, who was
planning to devote a substantial section of one issue of his ever-foraging journal *Ironwood* to works by Language Writers. He wanted a "critical" view of the action from a
sympathetic writer who was sufficiently intrigued to know much of the work, yet remained peripheral. I resisted his invitation for months but finally wrote the piece in an
effort to sort out my own ambivalent feelings. I knew my point-of-view would be seriously misread by some. It was.

of my vocabulary. I was not, at that point, responding to a new set of dictates. What I liked was the intrigue—the appearance of a "poem" with some of its various conventions (internal and end rhymes, linearity, recognizable musical figures, surprising moments of syntax and diction), undercut by a deliberate displacement of expected word orders and combinations. I was being given a code to break, complete with lyric outbursts and covert strategies meant to dash any idea I had of immediately understanding the writing in front of me. My habits were called into question. I was being asked to participate, to re-imagine what "stoves," "border," "lair" might mean in this context. And there was song. I recognized what pleasure that gave me. Tom said, when I asked him about it, that "L IN R" was, among other things, a love poem.

•

Most independent thinkers know the frustration of having limits dictated by others whose station in life gives them the power to imprint upon the community the good/bad appropriateness of a certain social, political, or aesthetic set of values or behaviors: admiring only "admired" works of art. What's been proposed as finally significant does not satisfy. Out of this, comes the next. One person's privately held challenge to the status quo links to others, springs into a dialogue or a publicly asserted political ideology, a new school of painting, a literary movement. At this point, a curious or dissatisfied person may wonder: is there something in this next new thing with which I can open up my own work?

•

These are notes on Language Writing, a phenomenon that has made one of its primary homes in the Bay Area poetry community over the last five years. This writing proposition has been discussed among poets here who, like flu victims struck in their vital parts, are unable to shake the new life form. A certain loss of equilibrium . . . then, adaptations.

I live in San Francisco and teach at San Francisco State—a university known for its political activism. I live among my friends the poets, the philosophers, the Feminists, the Marxists, the Heavy Metal progressives (my fifteen-year-old son and his musician friends). Each sub-community, each whole, includes a multiple of differences to distinguish its parts. Most of the above think and argue, distance and regroup continuously. Most of them are serious and are actively resisting the pull of tremendous cultural lag.

•

Entropy. Nuclear build-up. Worn-out language.

•

It began happening last year. Instead of poems lightly disguised as the ghosts of Robert Bly, Robert Creeley, or Adrienne Rich, I began getting some poetry assignments written in collaged fragments or sentences or paragraphs juxtaposed in amusing and unexpected ways . . . a more distanced, heady relationship to the writing, cutting back on the more obvious preoccupations with Self. I knew Language Writing had arrived. My poet friend, Bob Glück, who also teaches, said of similar student efforts: "They don't even know who they are being influenced by . . . but it's in the air."

He was right, but not about all of them. Some of them did know who. Clearly there was something very timely, necessary, and attractive about what the new writing and theory was proposing. And it was fun to write in sentences, to be liberated from the emotional tones of high lyricism and the fussiness of the line, to deprogram around poetry and to play with language as though it were unholy. This was the next deconstructive push, following various paths set forth earlier by certain of the New York School poets—doing their inventive part in the spirit of Baudelaire, Dada, Kurt Schwitters and André Breton—and experimentalists like John Cage and Jackson Mac Low who had introduced techniques of arbitrary mathematical patterning to break open syntactical habit and thought frame.

•

These notations propose themselves as a cluster of observations made at the interface of a complex but established writing community in the Bay Area and a new writing movement taking root in its midst. I have read some of the literature, not all of it. (There is a great deal.) I have attended many talks, readings and performances identified with language-centered writing. I have been, by turns, intrigued, bored, seriously engaged, wary. I have let it seep into the fiber, the pattern of my thoughts about the writing process/product. It has filtered, intentionally and unintentionally, into my writing. I have introduced many examples of Language Writing into the poetry writing workshops I teach, believing it to be serious, provocative, stimulating to the writing process, and broadly political in its implications. Still, I'm not a total convert.

.

ECHO is a transcript I made (slightly edited) from a tape of a performance I did at the Washington Project for the Arts as part of the Festival of Disappearing Arts on May 1, 1979. It opens with a reading of the poem "Echo" and a spontaneous monologue, and it goes on through increasingly improvisationally derived readings of things I had written and consecutive reworkings of that monologue listened to through earphones or speakers from tape, moving between the brick wall and the audience (this time in tiers) among my tape recorders, the things I'd written, and ladders. (Steve Benson's remarks, 1981, introducing a performance of "ECHO")

.

we get to shining apples making time go by till 5:30

when I go home. Staring off my business suit at the sunset

fading cloud incessant dream

and unstrap the curtains from the walls. Hit me over the head with your shovel and demand I scoop more sand into the bucket.

Your eyes are watershot and you've got a pubescent erection.

Your nose is turned like a hawk's, you're afraid I won't play fair. Is this, like everything else I'm told, about love,

hate, fear, funny?

I'm saying I'm in love, hearing it funny. The echo is blundered.

(Benson 1981, excerpt from "ECHO")

Steve Benson is the second person whose language-centered writing put me on alert. The quoted lines from "ECHO" illustrate his use of shifting pronouns, letting "I" travel into "you" or "we," so as to not remain static: how we try on other people and are never consistently one "I."

This is one way Steve puts language on paper. He also has written in a series of complete sentences or paragraphs, sometimes with discrete words or fragments falling in carefully composed (random seeming) patternings down the page. His work takes on increased tension in performance, involving his audience in the struggle to speak and to make choices. His use of movement—simple but intentional changes of body position as he's reading—makes you listen differently, alerts you, as in theater, to voice(s). He has used double mikes to underscore a continuous change-of-mind that may blurt into speech at the same time his taped voice (static, set text) is talking or reading . . . thus a juxtaposition of a live, improvised voice trying to comment on and respond to who "he" was "then"—the versions of "he" who *were,* when the taped text was being written and later spoken into the machine.

This *showing* of his process involves considerable personal risk in front of the audience. While Steve's constructions show a high degree of composition and control, he always leaves a space for the potentially out-of-control material to be active. His work admits to the dialectical process going on constantly within any thinking person. He is located, always, in the body as well as the intellect . . . and he is inevitably funny. I try not to miss his performances because I feel included in his questions and self-doubt. I am released, again, into the human community of speech. I go home needing to write.

·

In his essay "Continuous Reframing," the linguist George Lakoff brings over from the field of linguistics the concept of "the frame" in order to examine certain formal elements in recent works by the Bay Area performance artist, George Coates. Lakoff's comments are useful in understanding much of what is intended in the works of "Language" writers. He begins by explaining that:

We make sense of our experiences by categorizing them and fram-

ing them in conventional ways. A frame . . . is a holistic structuring
of experience. Each frame comes with a setting, a cast of characters, a collection of props, and a number of actions, states, and/or
images. . . . One typical kind of frame is a scenario for a cultural
event: a wedding, lecture, or football game. . . . Framing requires
categorizing; the objects, characters, images, and events must all be
of the right kind to fit a given frame . . . most of it done so continuously and unconsciously that we don't notice it.

Frame-shifting is . . . not merely a shift from one frame to another,
but from the frameable to the unframeable and back . . . a scenario
may be partially frameable as an attack by two characters upon a
third, but various aspects of the attack frame will be left unfilled—
who the characters are, their relationship, the motivation for the
attack. . . . The partialness of the framing is part of the art form, and
an indispensable part, since this kind of art requires the audience
to try constantly to categorize and frame, while never being totally successful. Things unframed gradually become framed, and
through the piece there is at each moment some partial framing
or other. It is this *partial local coherence* that holds the piece together
and that constantly holds our attention. (Lakoff 1982)

One objection to much of Language Writing has been that it is "elitist,"
particularly in its extensive body of theoretical writing. It has often been
understood or misunderstood as being meaningful only to persons with
extremely sophisticated linguistic preoccupations. One might ask, for example, whether a piece by Ron Silliman containing in one short passage
the terms "formalist/constructivist," "melopoiea," "exogamic determin-
ants" and "organicist" might not be off-putting to some readers, warily
framed as academic and overly infatuated with its own delicious brew of
rhetoric (*Soup* 2:45).

Other readers have been grateful for Silliman's attempt to illuminate
the somewhat removed category of poetry with structures adapted from
linguistic and Marxist theory (and their vocabularies), tangential, in his
mind, to every aspect of that formal thing called *poem,* as it is viewed

within the social/historical context from which we are all formed, to which we are all responsible.

·

Birthday Present
    for Carla Harryman
Dear _____,
The name They dropped on my face would intoxicate me,
perfumes, buzzed whispers, crotch and vine, smoke
with water, I dissect the Play.
    And They can put words with my Dolls, threading my
inspiration and respiration, green leaves and dry leaves,
hay in the barn, half unconscious, water the country
church is finished using.
    But This time, consciously, it is in my mouth, I see,
dance, sing, stout as a horse, repeated layers, full noon
trill exactly the contents of one, exactly the contents of two.
    O I perceive after all a boundless space, minor streams
beat time, the blab of the ear, red faced, ravished
fathomless condition with one small Diadem.
    I guess it must be the flag of my disposition, earth
bearing the owner's name brushed into the corners, I
behold the picturesque giant, the four horses, the beach.
    But this time, with Will to choose, to own the ear, to
stun the privilege and the same old law, walk five
friendly matrons, crowned, crowing.
    The pure contralto sings in the organ loft.
    Love, _____
        (Perelman 1981, "Birthday Present," 62)

In this poem, Bob Perelman has collaged lines or phrases from Emily Dickinson and Walt Whitman (perhaps others) inside his own visual and rhythmic writing. Part of the assumed pleasure of reading his "code" is dependent upon privileged information. Citations from the original poems are erased as part of the aesthetic post-modern claim to non-ownership, seen also in the practice of "sampling."

•

BARRETT WATTEN:"I don't like it when people speak for me. So it makes me not want to speak for myself, almost."

BOB PERELMAN:"Well, I *am* trying to speak for myself. . . . I identify quite a lot with Williams, especially the early Williams and his growls and anger at the amount of prerecording in his head. There's the sense of language being prerecorded and language acts as being spontaneous."

WATTEN: "One thing you get with O'Hara is a clear conflict between literature as learned in school and the interpretation of these conventions in the actual I, his actual I. O'Hara reinterprets literary forms in terms of the subjective I. But he doesn't propose that subjective I as the final result. There's a conflict all the way through that makes his I active. I think we owe a lot to that."

. . . .

WATTEN:"In writing, you want a world in which you live . . . you want to extend the borders of your world through the pronoun into the texts that are available to you. You want extension through the text and the main point of extension is through the pronoun."*

•

The appearance of a book of poems, if it be a book of good poems, is an important event because of relationships the work it contains will have with thought and accomplishment in other contemporary reaches of the intelligence. This leads to a definition of the term "good." If the poems in the book constitute necessary corrections of emendations to human conduct in their day, both as to thought and manner, then they are good. But if these changes originated in the poems, causing thereby a direct liberation of the intelligence, then the book becomes of importance to the highest degree. . . .

---

* Bob Perelman and Barrett Watten, from a conversation following Perelman's April 1979 talk, "The First Person." It was later published in Perelman's journal, *Hills* 6/7 (1980).

But this importance cannot be in what the poem says. . . . Its existence as a poem is of first importance a technical matter, as with all facts, compelling the recognition of a mechanical structure. . . . It is the acceptable fact of a poem as a mechanism that is the proof of its meaning and this is as technical a matter as in the case of any other machine. . . . Without the poem being a workable mechanism in its own right, a mechanism which arises from, while at the same time it constitutes the meaning of, the poem as a whole, it will remain ineffective. (Williams, quoted in Silliman 1981)

.

I had seen my political development mature to the point where I began seriously to doubt the appropriateness of my writing poetry for the consumption of a restricted class of highly educated, mostly white individuals; my political friends like to note the "elitism" of my work. . . . The audience I was building for my poetry was class-specific and I decided instead to attempt to make *that* the formal issue of my future work, demonstrating to it how both the class and its reality were (in part) constructed *through* language. . . . This led naturally to an investigation of the sentence and a critique of the use of lines in poetry. . . . It amounts to a shifting perception of the role of form as an aspect of any element in modern life, specifically as an *index of labor.*

All these issues have crucial analogues at the level of language itself. For example, the perception that the very presence of the line is the cheapest signifier of The Poetic now ongoing, will cause some people to abandon, at least for a time, its use. This, in turn, requires a new organizational strategy constructed around a different primary unit. To date, two major candidates have been proposed: (1) prose works built around investigations of the sentence (tho Watten's paragraph is an interesting variation); (2) the page itself as unit with "desyntaxed" words or phrases operating in a two-directional (at least) field. (Silliman 1979, 2)

·

It was only a   The tree rows in orchards are
coincidence   capable of patterns. What were
                         Caesar's battles but Caesar's prose. A
                         name trimmed with colored
                         ribbons. We "took" a trip as if that
were part of the baggage we carried. In other words, we "took
our time." The experience of a great passion, a great love, would
remove me, elevate me, enable me at last to be both special and
ignorant of the other people around me, so that I would be free
at last from the necessity of appealing to them, responding to
them. That is, to be nearly useless but at rest.

(Hejinian, 45)

·

Enacting Language Writing's device of appropriation and extension,
Hejinian adapts a visual move from Virginia Woolf's *A Writer's Diary*, bor-
rowing the "window space" carved from the left margin — as Woolf often
used it in her diary entries between 1925 and 1940 — to set apart a kind of
"title" or comment in apposition to the main text of each section of the
book-length serial poem *My Life*. Silliman, focusing on its mathematically
devised method of composition, describes the poem's plan this way:

> *My Life* is a single work: 37 paragraphs each with 37 sentences. In
> addition, each paragraph has a title or caption, sentences and phrases
> which themselves are repeated often throughout the text. My
> understanding is that the book was constructed cumulatively, with
> Hejinian originally writing a one-sentence paragraph, then a two-
> sentence paragraph and adding another sentence to the first, then
> a three-sentence paragraph, adding a new sentence to each of the
> first two paragraphs, etc. (Silliman, from his introductory remarks
> at a reading in San Francisco)

Silliman is introducing Lyn Hejinian's work to an audience that he has
very systematically worked to help create for writers now identified with

this movement. Hejinian had been writing and publishing in a variety of magazines for years before she was claimed as a Language Writer. Her own Tuumba series of chapbooks helped to create and sustain an audience of readers for experimentalist writing. In her public role on the National Endowment for the Arts Literature panel, between 1978 and 1981, she was a significant force in calling attention to bi-coastal writing projects from both new and established poets not part of the American mainstream.

L=A=N=G=U=A=G=E magazine, published and edited by Charles Bernstein and Bruce Andrews (between 1978 and 1981), focused interest on theoretical explorations of language experiment—and the socio/political conditions that had helped to create this work—while collecting and naming what Bernstein has called "a swirl of poetic activities . . . less unity than engaged conversation and exchange" (from a letter to the author, 1998).

Other journals and small presses important to the assertion and definition of language-centered writing include *BIG DEAL,* edited by Barbara Baracks; *La Bas* and, later, *Sun & Moon* (first a magazine, then a press), editor Douglas Messerli; *The Difficulties,* edited by Tom Beckett; *Open Letter,* edited by Frank Davey (with significant input from Steve McCaffery and bp Nichol); *A Hundred Posters,* edited by Alan Davies; *Shirt,* edited by Ray DiPalma; *THIS,* edited by Barrett Watten (first issue co-edited with Robert Grenier); *Qu,* edited by Carla Harryman; *miam,* edited by Tom Mandel; *Hills,* edited by Bob Perelman; *Tottel's,* edited by Ron Silliman; *Gnome Baker,* edited by Madeleine Burnside and Andrew W. Kelly; Tuumba Press, editor Lyn Hejinian; Awede Press, editor Brita Bergland; The Figures Press, editors Laura Chester and Geoff Young; Burning Deck Press, editors Keith and Rosmarie Waldrop; Segue and Roof Books, editor James Sherry; and Pod Books, editor Kirby Malone.

Robert Grenier's poems have been germinal to the thinking about and visualizing of word, syllable, juxtaposition, spatial relation of words to white page. Editor of Robert Creeley's *Selected Poems,* his own work was not widely appreciated until Language Poetry identified him and thus added to the legitimacy of his labors.

AWNING
yawning & yep
yawing & yamming
(Grenier 1980)

.

A respectful abstinence from knowing what I'm doing? There-
fore, my style seems to have fallen apart, deteriorated in the three
year interim between books; some kind of decadence has set in; it
has become problematical, not to say impossible, because if it limits itself to the traditional language & form of a literature it misses
the basic truths about itself, while if it attempts to tell those truths
it abolishes itself as literature. Chiastic sentence: not true, MAKE IT
NEW, caps, has always been the case, it's what literature means,
should mean. (Bromige 1980)

.

Some names often seen in Language Writing journals: *West Coast:* Barrett
Watten, Ron Silliman, Bob Perelman, Bob Grenier, Lyn Hejinian, Steve
Benson, Carla Harryman, Tom Mandel, Kit Robinson, Alan Bernheimer,
Rae Armantrout, Jean Day. *East Coast:* Bruce Andrews, Charles Bernstein,
Peter Seaton, James Sherry, Diane Ward, Nick Piombino, Alan Davies,
Michael Gottlieb, Steve McCaffery, Ray DiPalma, Peter Inman, Tina
Darragh, Lynne Dreyer, Doug Lang, Christopher Dewdney. Writers tan-
gential to and preceding it in their own unique ways: Clark Coolidge,
Larry Eigner, David Bromige, Michael Palmer, Michael Davidson, David
Antin, Stephen Rodefer, Ted Greenwald, Susan Howe, Hannah Weiner,
Jackson Mac Low, Bernadette Mayer, Rosmarie and Keith Waldrop.

.

Some important theoretical figures for Language writers: Louis Zukofsky,
Roland Barthes, Ferdinande de Saussure, Jacques Derrida, Ludwig
Wittgenstein, Walter Benjamin, the Russian Formalists—particularly Ro-
man Jakobson, Osip Brik (The Moscow Linguistic Circle) and Victor
Shklovsky, Boris Eichenbaum, Lev Jakubinsky and the OPOYAZ group—
acronym for the Society for the Study of Poetic Language, based in St.
Petersburg around 1916 (Watten 1980, 51).

.

After the initial period, in which the Bay Area was actively enriched with new little magazines and small presses and a proliferation of readings exclusively programmed with the above names—a period in which the audience was largely self-supporting and self-referring—the effect of Language Writing began to be felt in the larger arts community. The news of its collective enterprise began to spread and audiences have grown. On a typical evening, you can find—in addition to its hard-core practitioners—ten to fifteen established poets who are interested but not affiliated, plus a growing number of young writers and students, some from the visual arts community.

Many people have wanted to try on this new identity, others have felt dismissed or limited by its poetics. Still others have seen in what was proposed as a political and community-based movement, a more exclusive (thus excluding) social group of writers—mostly straight, white, male, linguistically oriented, who appeared to be interested primarily in each other's works and in inscribing the next new tablets of stone.

But doesn't any new movement function in much this way? To reconnoiter, to report on a collective vision (with its inevitable differences and dissonances), to support each other in the active working out of that commitment—in this case, the remaking of a language usage and poetics that no longer adequately serves their artistic or social needs. No one can dispute the fact that Language Writers have labored tirelessly to make a place for their passionate concerns, a forum (always open to anyone interested) for arguing the philosophical and practical questions that are central to their commitment as writers. They assume their questions to be useful to the larger writing community. This has proved to be true. And from their perspective they have been, in Steve Benson's words: "a bunch of writer friends who have, through mutual challenge and encouragement, developed striking sophistication and discipline in responding to concerns of some consistently common interest. . . ."

Still, ambivalence toward upper-case Language Writing exists in many women whose writing history had been, until the early Seventies, formed largely by male teachers, editors, and critics whose tastes conformed to experiences, aesthetic values, pleasures, and struggles *as* men in a social/

political world where access to power and print was assumed. A growing awareness of this suddenly glaring fact—its clout and assumption of the word—has posed serious questions for women writers who struggle for language access to their own experience: To what extent has our experience been suppressed or examined exclusively through the finely polished lens of the male writing sensibility? What qualities of perception, what moments of importance may have been devalued consistently by the *absence* of a significant body of writing by women that might have reinforced a reality that did not find validation in the bulk of literature brought forward in textbook choices—the literary canon.

These sorts of questions have formed the basis of a developing feminist poetics that shares an ambition common to Language Writing—that is, to reinvent, deconstruct, find syntactical and experiential detours out of the dominant and often turgid mainstream. But there is an understandable wariness in simply following the diagrams and preferences of the new language formalists who are, once again, male-dominant in their *theoretical* documents. It would seem as urgent and more interesting, really, for many a woman writer to attend first to the unraveling of her own buried history of/in language before it gets classified, theorized, tamed.

One needs to listen, as well, to the inner prompt and then to write from the fragments and layerings of incoherence, unsureness, even extreme vulnerability. While the structural preoccupations of language-centered theory and practice are stimulating and concretely useful, the aesthetic distaste for *any* self-referentiality introduces (yet again) the concept of prohibition. For a writer whose awareness has been tuned by the growing need to claim her own history and present tense, Language Writing's directives are often encountered—if not intended—as the newest covenant.

Still, there is often a feeling of friendly curiosity and mutual regard for this common project: initiating one's own alternatives to what has thus far been proposed as the whole of significant poetry. The shift is apparent, the aesthetic mandate infinitely more complex.

·

Language generates reality in the inescapable context of power.

—Donna Harraway

Faulty Copying

Error lay at the source of all change, all species experiment. It was the author of all the still emerging undesignable variations on life. . . . The ability of traits to persist in stillness. Evolution is the exception, stability the rule. . . . yet faulty copying [of genetic information] is the only agency for change. . . . Species laugh off the most rigorous hierarchy. . . . The aim is to widen the target, to embrace more than was possible before.

> —Richard Powers, *The Gold Bug Variations*

. . . who works at his [her] own word in all of our sentences might trick from even the ruts of once ritual the buts and mistakes that token the actual. The poet as maker frees the thing from its prophets.

> —Robert Duncan, footnote in "Letters for Denise
> Levertov: An A Muse Ment"

From as early in my life as I can remember, I resisted others' categories and imperatives, perhaps because there were so many of them. I didn't like being identified too readily or absolutely, nor did I wish to represent anything that could be described ahead of time. One of the first poems I wrote—around 1963—was called "Change of Address" (Fraser 1966, 4) in which the poet is seen to survive the mistaken and shifting identities of a quick-change artist. My poem was refusing a world that, in the early Sixties, seemed to press upon me its definitions of writing and the writer's

FRAME: In the winter of 1993, I was invited by Charles Bernstein to do a short residency as a guest of the Poetics Program at SUNY Buffalo. My stay would include a formal talk to Bernstein's graduate poetics seminar, so I took the occasion to write about error in DNA and typography—how error began to appear and then to figure consciously in my poems beginning around 1980. This essay was originally published under the title "This Phrasing Unreliable Except as Here" in *Talisman* 13 (1994).

task a bit too unconditionally for my comfort. I was barely climbing out of an extended adolescence and a well-meaning family and religious community in which others' confident plans for me bore little resemblance to the writing consciousness forming at its own speed inside me. My maturing process was not going according to anyone's plan, least of all my own.

My map kept changing; nothing would stay in place. The only principle that seemed reliable was my unreliability in predicting what I would pursue and how that might manifest itself. That early conviction of unreliability in the narration of my own "voice" shifted more radically as my exposure to the peculiar and various dictions of American poetry created a stimulating havoc in my forming poetics.

But it's not quite true to say that I *never* wanted to represent anything I could describe ahead of time. Part of whatever made up my particular family imprint pulled at me regularly throughout my midwestern Calvinist upbringing, doing its best to move me forwards in the direction of various ideals of rationality and perfection. In the effort to attain those plateaus of excellence, so much was never said.

My mother and father came from families wishing to conform to the dictates they understood as the guarantee of a safe and respectable life, even though their most memorable acts were rash attempts to escape that life. They inherited this burden of survival behavior with a good deal of grace *and* ambivalence, demonstrating when at all possible admirable strategies for fanciful escape. Language was the field and the ground for that demonstration. We had very little money to spend on average consumer pleasures, but we always had drawing and singing and books; and because we had books there was an immense freedom among us to intrigue and amuse one another with three-dimensional cross-pollinations of useless nonsense verse, silly song lyrics, little-known or imagined facts and unsolved mysteries. I learned early that my best escape route from tedium and the oppressive cloud of convention was the tunnel into language. In word tunnels you could dig your way out.

Perhaps it is because of that old and persistent tug that I want to address the issue of perfection versus error, to describe where error has taken me—its unreliable path—and what error has given me, in the act of writing, that the goal of "perfection" cannot.

·

But what does perfection mean in this context? *Webster's Unabridged,* second edition, defines it as: "1. the act or process of perfecting; as, the perfection of the machine took many months. 2. the quality or condition of being perfect; the extreme degree of excellence according to a given standard. 3. A person or thing that is the perfect embodiment of some quality."

In poetry, perfection implies at the least a pre-existing model of writing practice, a model of structural aptitude and acclaimed excellence as well as a particular stylistic signature that has been named, admired, and awarded the serious attention of a like community. It follows that one's consciously chosen or inadvertent models of "perfection" could as well be based upon Duchamps' word pieces as Horace's *Odes,* Emily Dickinson's lyrics as Lorine Niedecker's condensed reflective tercets.

It is the paradigm, its pre-existence and public presence that allows one to find this model or "voice," latch on to it, and even, in some cases, merge with it. True love. It is what you needed to get you started on your own linguistic trajectory—and it seems to satisfy you for the moment, such merging. But this form of admiration and stimulation is like the originating scientist's experiment being verified again and again by colleagues in the field, using the precise measurements and problems set forth by the person who first posed the particular question and put in long lab hours watching endless petri dishes for the division of cells said experiment necessitated. Participation in verification is instructive and reassuring; one learns to move more confidently in the lab. But the staging of a new observation, its tracery not yet revealed, hovers as another order of experience.

Stability's prediction versus eruption's change of pace. Photogenic versus pathogenic. Information passing, as in genetic instruction on how to make a hair color or a sintence . . . I mean a sentence. Except that some segment of instruction is often accidentally waylaid, one little piece of the chemical code misfired. Faulty copying. This is either good chemistry or bad, depending on whether you're looking for formal replication as your goal or are more interested in inadvertent revision, the potential syntactic manifestation. Cell-division poetics. When the Nobel Prize was given out in the fall of 1993, the American research scientist, Phillip A. Sharp, and an English scientist, Richard J. Roberts, divided a prize for their simultaneous discovery of "split genes" that foreshadowed the development of massive discoveries in genetic engineering technology. What interested me was that both these men began their quest by looking for something other than what they found. They began with a familiar, scientifically sanctioned theoretical base and set of research procedures, working with adenoviruses that cause common colds. They attempted to identify the locations of individual genes in this virus because it was assumed by the scientific establishment that these adenovirus genes shared important similarities with those of higher organisms. That is, they began with a preexisting model as the basis of their hunt. But as the *Los Angeles Times* reported, "To their surprise, they found that each gene was not located at one discrete site but was spread out over a large region interspersed with sections—now called introns—of so-called nonsense DNA with *no discernible function . . .*" (my italics). Many other researchers quickly scrambled to show that genes of most other organisms, up to and including human beings, have a similar organization.

Sharp and Roberts's discovery also provided new insight into evolution. Researchers had previously believed that "evolution occurred when *single* chemicals in a gene mutated, producing subtle changes in the protein for which the gene is a blueprint." But their new research showed, instead, that "the accumulation of many such changes over a long period of time was thought to be necessary for a significant change in the function of a protein." The metaphoric implications of this discovery are not lost on those of us who are writers.

How is it that the scrubbed and well-brushed formulae of The Known so often begin as our internalized judges in both the sciences and the arts, apart from any intention of the poem or the cell's functioning to represent any final paradigm? Does that "perfect" static resting place, often regarded as "the prize-winning solution," actually function as the carrot dangling from the stick, the lure urging us forward with its possibility of temporary sustenance so that we may go on to risk our own idiosyncratic depictions and commit our own perfection-resistant "errors"?

·

The first piece of writing in which I consciously chose to incorporate the sight and citing of a literal error or "typo" as interesting information and legitimate poetic material was in "this. notes. new. year." written on December 26, 1979 (Fraser 1980, 11–13; 1998, 39–41). The second paragraph of this piece is marked as an "aside," a shift of narrating voice set apart by parentheses:

> (She was "in a fury" and she wept in spite of herself. His letter told the usual stories in all the old ways. She swallowed them whole. Then came the nausea. She wanted a "flow" she thought, but in the translation it was corrected, displacing the *o* and substituting *a*. She could give herself to an accident. She was looking out the window.) (Fraser 1998, 39)

This involuntary error of *a* in place of *o,* made during the typing of the phrase "She wanted a 'flow' "—and the subsequent attention to the shape-shift that "flaw" dictated—changed the path of my investigation. It gave me a kind of freedom to interrogate a wider terrain than I'd imagined at the beginning of the writing, so that what and whom I'd originally imagined as my speaking subject was allowed to become unreliable, and more interesting to me as receiver/transmitter.

.

The next work I'm aware of, in this context, is one in which an error provided the title for the poem "boundayr." The text of the poem had been produced through a sort of call-and-response method borrowed from jazz improvisation in which I began with the primary colors blue, red, and yellow—the "calls" or points of focus around which associations (or "responses") magnetized. From that core of three, I let my eye wander around the room in which I sat, randomly seizing upon each color that suggested itself, naming it and waiting for the association to arrive. Clearly, this method was not directed by a conscious personal or emotional agenda except for the compelling need to write. Reading through the text after retyping it, I noticed that I'd accidentally transposed the last two letters of the word "boundary" so that instead the typo "boundayr" took its place. I was fascinated, without attaching any particular significance to the new meaning suggested by the mistaken spelling, but decided to use that error as an intentional title because I liked its visual surprise. Only weeks later did I see that without consciously intending it, the impersonal structure of color association had released into the text a tissue of disquietude and dissatisfaction with the emotional and intellectual parameters of a life that felt—at the moment—shut down, almost as if the air itself were binding me in some unseen vise. The "boundayr" typo both located this condition and became the voicing of it, as well as the impetus to break free from that bind . . . a familiar theme for me, as it turned out.

.

The third example in my work, wherein the crime of error is committed and then pursued in order to bring to light a code or body of clues hidden in the text, is in the poem "La La at the Cirque Fernando, Paris" (Fraser 1998, 158 – 68). I would like to trace the poem's points of initiation, as they involuntarily gathered in me during a trip to the Normandy coast of France in February 1988. On that journey, I visited the famed cathedral and island fortress of Mont St. Michel, a rough island-like rock promontory—also the site of a tiny community of dwellings and shops separated from the mainland of France by the flat gray and forbidding waters of the incoming tide.

I'd been reading Henry Adams's architectural history, *Mont St. Michel and Chartres,* in preparation for better appreciating the cathedral's uniquely embodied architectural shift from Romanesque to Gothic. As part of this reading, I had gleaned all sorts of fascinating details about the daily life of the Normandy fisherfolk, their habits, rituals and songs. One bit I copied into my reading journal was a couplet quoted in Adams:

> Who reads me, when I am ashes,
> Is my son in wishes. . . .
> (Adams 1986, preface)

Its origin was credited as "Some old Elizabethan play or poem," and it later found its way into my poem.

Approaching the isolated and near-mythic fortress structure of Mont St. Michel over an extended distance of flat land gave one a chance to take it in, at first, as a kind of hovering dream image. As we drew closer, we could see the magnificent golden figure lifting off the top-most cathedral spire, facing south: it was the figure of St. Michel (Saint Michael), patron saint of France, sword raised above his head in an eternal gesture of both victory and guardianship. One could easily imagine the daily imprint of this powerful young male protector upon the imaginations of women who worked in the sand marshes just at the base of the cathedral, collecting the rough-shelled *fruits d'mer* at every low tide to sell at nearby market towns.

My companion and I became so fascinated by Adams's pilgrimage to the various Normandy cathedrals that, after we'd explored Mont St. Michel's soaring ribs and spires, we followed Adams's trail to Avranches, Coutances, and Caen to look at other examples of Romanesque/Gothic hybrids, along the way visiting the bitterly cold seacoast village of Honfleur with its bustling farmer's market in the town square. An old fellow was selling more than 105 kinds of local cheese from the twig baskets arranged on his table. Near him, others sat with buckets of sea urchins and every kind of shellfish; also tables were piled with the leafy winter green called *betterave* (our beetroot). In the café where we went to warm our hands, the barkeep poured the traditional Normandy apple brandy called *Calvados*.

These local details unknowingly collected in me so that by the time we reached our final destination, the physical ground for a piece of writing was well into preparation. The triggering image that connected the St. Michel material to the poem was a painting by Degas, reproduced on a postcard that I found during the first day of our airing-out the apartment we would live in for the next few months. Apparently the card had slipped from a wall and lay under the bed, gathering dust. Its reproduced painting, "La La at the Cirque Fernando, Paris," shows a young female circus performer hanging by her teeth from a ring at the top of a domed, turn-of-the-century circus gallery in Paris. I'd looked at that postcard reproduction many times the year before, although I'd never made much of a connection beyond its pleasurable surface of colors and suggested subject. But coming upon it so unexpectedly after the Normandy trip, I found myself thinking about the circus girl, La La, wondering how she might have arrived at that suspended place. A kind of fictional/imaginal process took over, its telling initially dictated through a more lyric or song-like narrative, rather than the low-key prose inflections of a poetics fueling my work since the mid-Seventies. It was as if La La's story took possession of me, her tonalities and necessity to speak from her own life taking precedence over "my" poetic identity, as "I" might have described it at that moment in 1988.

The opening lyric narrative tells of La La's seduction by a traveling circus man, Fernando, who lures her into the glamorous adventure of center-stage by teaching her how to grab the ring with her teeth and to twirl her body as he pulls her aloft. Such lyric writing seemed appropriate to this merging of Degas's nineteenth-century sensibility and the voice of a small-town country girl. Nevertheless, fairly deep into the handwritten first draft (say, section eight or nine), I began typing what had emerged, to see how it looked, and suddenly everything shifted gears. The error-prone writer in me, whose work had developed through the lens and practice of much formal experiment, began to engage. As I read the typescript and came to part four, called "The trick," I noticed a typo. I'd accidentally typed a capital *D* in the name "FernanDo." I liked the way it looked and decided to scan the text following that error and to consciously repeat and fore-ground the capitalized letter at the beginning of any word's final syllable, as it presented itself. I had nothing else in mind, reading swiftly along until a word moved out to me, its last syllable announcing a recognizably inde-pendent word. It took me a minute, at the most, to find these words inside of other words. They were: grimAce, betteRave, counTry, whirRing, beCalmed, townEdge, stageDoor, someOne's, presSure and swalLow. There were probably more, but those are the ones that caught my eye at the moment.

Another visual figure appeared, almost in parallel time with the above words. This was the grid-like figure I found in my dictionary while look-ing up the word "matrix," encountered in a separate, nonfiction psychol-ogy text I'd been reading while we were on the road. When I saw the twelve-station matrix/grid of *a, b, c, d,* crossed with 1, 2 and 3, I immedi-ately flashed on the words I'd gone back to capitalize inside of La La's narrative. I thought that if there were enough of them, they might provide an interesting crossword puzzle for her, something to do while Fernando was at the bar getting sloshed on Pernod. At the same time, I thought it might possibly provide her with a code as she began emerging from the state of speechless thralldom—Fernando's property—and moving into her own possession of language and selfhood.

When I counted the words, there were eleven. I needed one more to complete the grid. I looked in part nine and found the final two-syllable word, "surpRise." At that moment, the poem absolutely took off for me because when I read the matrix/grid, either as lines or as columns, it seemed to articulate an encoded version of La La's struggle into voice:

Matrix

a1 Do	b1 Ace	c1 Rave	d1 Try
a2 Ring	b2 Calmed	c2 Edge	d2 Door
a3 One's	b3 Sure	c3 Low	d3 Rise

Swiftly, the final *Coda* appeared, as if spoken directly out of her voice:

dear	arc	angel
have	broken	code
now	need	speech

(Fraser 1998, 167–68)

.

The last error-prone structure I wish to look at is "Giotto : ARENA," a work composed of seventeen parts.* By the time I came to the writing of this poem, the "problem" or potential meanings of error versus perfection had been unfolding in my mind for several years and had begun to take on a more conscious urgency. Beginning to think about Giotto's renegade project at the Arena Chapel in Padova, I found that I wanted to consciously stage and foreground the occasion of error—or otherness—in his work as intentional resistance to the art establishment of his day.

In my research, I had uncovered a fascinating history of the Arena Chapel,

---

* The poem originated as an *ABACUS 62* and was later included in *When New Time Folds Up* (Minneapolis: Chax Press, 1993): 49–69; and in *il cuore: the heart. Selected Poems, 1970–1995* (Middletown, Conn.: Wesleyan University Press, 1997): 119–37.

originally called the Scrovegno Chapel after the family whose name it takes.** The story is that the older Scrovegno, Reginaldo, was known for such avaricious money-lending practices that he was ostracized by the Catholic Church and thus denied its blessing at his death. Enrico Scrovegno, hoping to atone for his father's sins and to reinstate the Scrovegno family name within the Church's and the community's good graces, had the original family chapel razed and a new one built, to be dedicated to the Virgin Mary. He hired Giotto, by then the most admired young painter in Tuscany, to cover the entire interior of the Chapel with frescoes depicting scenes from the scriptures. (Dante, hearing of the local Padova gossip, no doubt from his friend Giotto, later featured the greedy Reginaldo in the seventh circle of *l'Inferno*.)

As I worked on this poem, I began to implant messages in the text through the placement of misspellings or extended approximations of familiar words. I also began to collage and reconstruct passages from Dante and John Ruskin, as a testing and questioning of any final authority, and to reinforce the poetic materials with typo/graphics including telegraphed bulletins, handwritten words, and marginalized fragments meant to elicit the reader's decoding of my reading of Giotto's Arena Chapel statement. It had become clear to me that the painting in these frescoes represented an immense shift away from the familiar depictions encoded in Byzantine art, turning definitively from the expectations of a critical establishment and church patronage that favored known replication—the perfectionism of art.

Reading about Giotto's life and artistic development and looking more closely at each of the panels covering the entire surface of the Arena Chapel's walls and ceilings, I began to understand the basis for his radical departure from the norm. As a young shepherd boy, his visual curiosity had been occupied with the close observation of animals and the terrain where they

---

** Texts referred to here include: Sevatico, *Sulla Cappellina degli Scrovegni nell'Arena de Padova* (Padova, 1836); Giorgio Vasari, *The Lives of Artists,* trans. George Bull (New York: Penguin, 1965); and John Ruskin, *Giotto and his Works in Padua* (London: George Allen, 1905).

grazed. Details fascinated him, the odd difference. He noticed the way sheep leaned together in a storm, how the rough spun fabric of shepherds' cloaks gathered shadow in its folds. When the master painter, Cimabue — walking north of Florence on a hill path near Giotto's village — found the nine-year-old boy drawing a sheep on a stone with a piece of campfire charcoal, he was immediately struck by the accuracy of detail and sought out Giotto's parents, offering to take on the boy as an apprentice in his Florence studio. Through years of tutelage, Cimabue encouraged Giotto to express his own way of seeing.

Giotto was able to break from the artistic conventions of his time because his attention had not been stylistically limited nor shaped by a predetermined idea of how a man's hair or a sheep's wooly coat *should* be represented. He was not required to negotiate a canon of preference — theoretical mandates, such as "the great system of perfect color" then being dictated to the artistic community by Byzantine scribes. Giotto's seeing was direct and his desire to paint his subject as he saw it, unswerving.

.

Idealized daily life was further dwelt upon by Ruskin in his discourse on translation — in this case, the Italian to English passage from Dante's *L'Inferno,* Canto xvii, translated by the Rev. Henry Francis Cary in 1805. Ruskin points out Cary's fear of Dante's homeliness of speech, revealing an unconscious denial of a probable class-based diction and rendering it more palatable to the upper bourgeoisie of England.

For example, in translating Dante's line "*un'oca piu bianca che burro*" (a goose more white than butter), the translator had smoothed it over into what *he* thought of as a more mellifluous (and comfortable) English, "whiter wing than curd." This intentional smoothing or editing away of what had been read by the translator/critic as a rougher style of articulation is just one historic link in the great chain of erasure and/or assertion of official aesthetic policy inextricably connected to the marginalization of *any* work that does not fit a current politics of assessment and agreement.

We know that the claim to perfection comes after the fact, dancing on the rooftop of the inverse pyramid that betokens popular agreement. But there is always someone who sees otherwise and proposes a shift in scale —

that something normally LARGE be reduced to one tenth its size or repeated five times; that a very slowly moving sequence of dots be speeded up; that a prismatic view of color be looked at in the dark. A name is given to that fresh angle, and the naming itself alerts the next buzz of interest.

Perhaps the illusion that we are acquainted with some fairly stable idea of what we want to represent and contribute to humanity's sum product during our lives as thinking/creating beings is what keeps us going, or is it the constant inner nagging that we haven't yet got it quite right? Illusion works to protect us, even as our self-doubt and self-critique become more refined, more persistent.

For me, any early conviction of how I wanted to write shifted over the years to a process based more in close scrutiny and attention to what was going on in the writing itself, how it changed and what the sources of those changes were, as the drafts of a piece opened up more variables. Accumulation and selection took on fascination. Perfect copying held less allure as I began to savor the reliability of the unexpected.

Part II

Missing . Persons

equilibrium
(cut her name
out of every
scribble)
hymn   himnal now, equal-
lateral

(KF, "re: searches," 1986)

Photogenes: "the incidental" & "the inessential" as modernist postscript

> She is defined and differentiated with reference to man and not he
> with reference to her; she is the incidental, the inessential as opposed
> to the essential. He is the Subject, the Absolute—she is the Other.
>
> —*The Second Sex,* Simone de Beauvoir

> Patriarchal she said what is it I know what it is it is I know I know so
> that I know what it is I know so I know so I know so I know what it
> is. Very slowly. I know what it is it is on the one side a to be her to be
> his to be their to be in an and to be I know what it is it is he who was
> an known not known was he was at first it was the grandfather then
> it was not that in that the father not of that grandfather then then she
> to be to be sure to be sure to be I know to be sure to be I know to be
> sure to be not as good as that.
>
> —from "Patriarchal Poetry," Gertrude Stein

The photogene is an after-image, an impression retained on the retina of
the eye after the object itself has vanished. It is as real in its visual hover as
its initiating agent, but is more ephemeral and cannot exist without the
image or "text" that preceded it. Trying to reassemble the photogenes of a
modernist vision or history without all the originating frames is problem-

---

FRAME : In 1993, Trudi Tate organized a conference on "Modernism: Politics, Poetics, Practice" at Cambridge University, Kings College. Susan Gevirtz, an American poet and Richardson scholar, was asked to put together a panel, and she invited me to participate. We collaborated on a title for the panel, to be called "Displacement as Intentional Critique: Contemporary Women's Poetry and Persisting Modern Practice" and wrote our papers with this in mind. At the last minute, we were asked to combine our panel with a second panel which seemed to be pursuing a distinctly different agenda. Although this change might have been potentially interesting, it upset the dynamic we'd been developing. As a result, the night before our departure for England I tabled the original form of my essay (here included) and collaged quite a different piece from the same resource materials. I will never know how it landed in the minds of the audience, but I later wished I'd read both versions.

atic—particularly where one's reading first intersected with a heavily re-vised version. It is a bit like chasing down a set of film-clips or outtakes of images and sections of script that were not included in the final cut of the film, for want of time or appraised box-office value. These frames, lacking use, are eventually discarded from the archive, only to be found years later at the bottom of a box in a locked metal cabinet—and often missing a soundtrack. Their remains may or may not be restored if deemed of value.

We've begun to understand what it is that we have in these partially reclaimed images, but what *might* have remained is still up for speculation. Incomplete possession of modernist photogenes means that significant origi-nating texts by modernist women poets and novelists simply didn't exist in our experience of reading and thinking about language as young Ameri-can writers in the Sixties and Seventies. What impact did this absence have, particularly on the life of a young woman poet unfinished in her forma-tion and uncertain of her fit into the larger world of poetry? Next to the scale and measure and finality of traditional verse—a mostly male career, as one had been given to understand it—most women's lives seemed to lack the significance of event defining those masterpieces selected for our texts and anthologies. Unknowingly, we existed in a state of suspension—linguistically sensitive writers waiting to be invited into our own century.

Until I heard Virginia Woolf's voices speaking in *The Waves,* I dutifully wandered along traditional paths, only partially realized as a reader among topiary forms of language, with no available structural models for locating the inarticulate clash in me between a speechlessness of resistance to tradition's burden and the multi-vocal escape from it.

Woolf's body of work comprises the first significant photogene in my modernist history and, if after-images carried soundtracks, I would suggest that her swarming voices—fragmented with "inessential" mutter and mur-mur and "incidental" reflections on the human psyche—have continued to give me access to that inner clamor of selves, its observations and argu-ments inside me. Her choral poetics—a counterpoint of digression—in-vited me into a writing practice that came to value idiosyncratic scrutiny, amplification, and subversion. Its demonstration of the overflowing pools and waves of de Beauvoir's *incidental* language invited a shift in my percep-tion of poetry as a gathering and developing investigation, breaking against

the tidy borders and end-stops of comfortable verse. It permitted the validity of female authority.

My debt to Woolf is, in part, a postscript. Only years later did I realize
that, except for her and for Dickinson, my twentieth-century poetic writing models had been exclusively male. The formal initiation into a read-
ing/writing world that American universities provided in the late Fifties/
early Sixties, included few texts by modernist women writers. At first, it
didn't seem to matter. Just about everything thrilled me with its newness.
I read early Joyce and encountered the poetic dictions of T. S. Eliot, e.e.
cummings, and William Carlos Williams. My introduction to modernism
had begun, complete with its erasure of major modernist women writers
who would not surface in my life for ten to twenty years. I did not yet
understand the undermining sense of otherness — of being incidental to
the essential production of a new literature — or what the *lack* of female-
authored innovative texts would engender in me, both as reader *and* forming writer looking for models of linguistic originality and artistic persistence.

Fortunately, the "inessential" life of female thought and perception and
the "incidental" fragmenting of Woolf's characters awakened in me a profound recognition: I identified immediately with the complex world she
was unraveling. Consequently, I began to *hear* and to give value to my own
interior life and to track the bifurcated, elaborate, interruptive speech of
my own company of selves. Woolf's writing engaged me in a process of
psychological identification and structural detection. A woman writer had
located and given voice to levels of existence I'd unconsciously denied as
worthy. Only in the late Seventies did I make the discovery of and connection between the immense and revolutionary labors of Dorothy
Richardson and of Woolf's subsequent breakthrough; that Woolf was enabled by her study of Richardson's sensibility and revolutionary technical
innovation to develop her own version of re-conjugating subjectivity and
amplifying a vast choral syntax of daily event.

This clarification was enlightening, but it had its discouraging subtext.
Soon enough, I was alerted to Woolf's unique social position in a circle of
culturally privileged men who supported her daily writing practice, almost as if playing the part of workers and drone to the queen until her

fertile product had been delivered. Yet even Woolf characterized women's mode of articulation as "a little language," describing it in *A Writer's Diary* as being "made up of small broken words, brief unfinished sentences, cries, calls, songs, silences, sights, and gestures" (quoted in Eisenberg 1981, 254). While identifying and including materials that substantiated a vastly expanded territory of female interiority, Woolf's description stood, nevertheless, as a delimiting claim. In some way it undermined its own liberating cry, even while delivering us from the singular privilege and power of the Queen Bee. It carried the ring of authority one had been conditioned to grant to a mostly male literary circle, yet compromised itself by suggesting a self-prescribed diminution for all women writers.

Perhaps it wouldn't have seemed quite that way — only one description of many — if the works of Dorothy Richardson or Djuna Barnes or Gertrude Stein or Ivy Compton Burnett had been on anyone's reading list or their writings even hinted at among a group of initiates. At the least, we would have had the idea of a plurality of innovative writing practices among modernist women. If the poetry of H.D., Laura Riding, Mina Loy, Mary Butts, and Lorine Niedecker had continued to circulate along with Williams, Pound, Stevens, and Zukofsky, the knowledge and pleasure of a richly diverse and linguistically inventive female poetics would have extended our ideas of what was being imagined, experienced, and forged in our century. Lamentably, these names stand in for photogenes that did not exist for me or thousands of other readers at that time. We were still being taught to read the world's codes through a limited authorship of mostly white male privilege.

Who erased the effective presence of so many modernist women writers, and *why*, is a slippery bit of research, but the after-image of lack remains even as one joins in the collective labor of restoration. In a conversation, in the mid-Seventies, with the American writer Mary Oppen — several generations my senior — she casually asked me if I'd read Dorothy Richardson. She was sure I would like her writing, knowing my interest in innovative forms, and was immensely surprised to find that I'd never been introduced to Richardson's twelve-volume fictional work, *Pilgrimage,* in a literature class. Soon after, the poet Barbara Guest brought up the name of Richardson again and I went hunting for *Pilgrimage* in the bookstores with no success. It was out of print and not to be found in the more sophisticated local libraries. Both writer friends had singled out this work with an urgent sense of recognition I'd seldom heard from my university professors. In that generational shift, Richardson's work had been allowed to disappear.

Current poetic exploration among American, Canadian, and British women in the last twenty years has shown an increasing debt to the modernist writers mentioned here. Their practice privileges partial knowledge and fragmentary perception as valid and valued evidence and works to resist closure, seeing uncertainty and marginality as a place from which to speak accurately.

Precisely because of this fragile and fairly recent path of regeneration, I am not yet ready to cut loose and move entirely away from certain of modernism's freeing strategies to a post-modern intervention against an "older generation." Though born generations earlier, the modernist women writers primarily entered our lifetime *after* such major American influences as Olson, Duncan, Creeley, Oppen, Zukofsky, O'Hara, and Ashbury had made their influence felt. In fact, many later writings by these male authors were strongly inflected and shaped by what they had learned from such earlier writers as Woolf and Stein and H.D.

I have just begun to engage with the difficult soundings of modernism's female half. I still need the wild humor of Stein's re-grammaring—its refusal to submit; Niedecker's tenacious, sinewy yet delicate poetic line and her mistrust of any language's tendency to dissemble; Riding's philosophic dark humor compressed to cut; Mina Loy's skeptical view of romantic codes, her flagrant sexual inventions; H.D.'s empowering permission to re-think myth or any exclusively male version of the story, her naming of the palimpsest form as a structural necessity.

The women modernists refused encapsulation & stratification, exposing class-invested models of formal purity and unity as party-line poetics. Not incidentally, each of them found a way, somehow, to go into a room and shut the door and work. But how much access do we, in fact, have to the work that was written behind those shut doors? Will missing outtakes of the central modernist script be doomed to permanent cold-storage? Will these photogenes remain sealed in their metal cabinets?

Letter from Rome: H.D., Spero, and the reconstruction of gender

These reflections have taken place in tandem with the opening of Nancy Spero's show, "Sky Goddess, Egyptian Acrobat," her first show in Rome at the Stefania Miscetti Gallery, an occasion almost parallel with the arrival of related Spero collages in *o.blek* 9. Said events have layered themselves with my rereading of H.D.'s *Trilogy*, and I've been newly struck by the connections between Spero and H.D.; how their methods both underscore and illuminate the territory recently explored by Amelia Jones in her piece, "The Absence of Body" (*M/E/A/N/I/N/G* 9).

Jones writes that "The literal breaking apart of the body of the 'enemy' is a means to annihilate by cutting off, refusing the flow that is perceived to run out of control in the body of the (m)other—feared (fantasized) as dangerously unbounded and threatening to male order" (14). I remember, as I read, a particularly devastating photo-image used by Spero depicting a woman, head turned down and away from the camera, mouth gagged, her naked body entirely bound with rope so that you can see it pressing into

---

FRAME: This letter-essay was written in response to a piece I read in *M/E/A/N/I/N/G* 9 (1991), a feminist/visual arts journal and forum (New York City) whose stance was critical to—and of—mainstream arts community practices. Its co-editors, Mira Schor and Susan Bee, kindly sent my subscription to Rome where I had—just days before—been profoundly struck by a group of Nancy Spero works hung for a show in one of the old and dramatically high-ceiling'd buildings one finds in the *centro storico*. This, plus a serendipitous re-reading of H.D.'s *Trilogy*, provoked the need to explore the difference between what is newly made and how it is often hyped (and displaced) with old rhetoric and dangerous romanticism.

her flesh, as if to cut off or forcibly contain some dangerous flow or current. This cut-out photo is reproduced by Spero twice—once in dark shadow and, again to its right and slightly higher, the same photograph is lit in harsh detail, underscored with the newsprint caption "*Document trouve sur un membre de La Gestapo.*" This collage is one marker in Spero's effort to re-embody the lost female history of "mankind." By making her viewer look at this image, she takes it out of the Gestapo's pocket, exposing *and* refusing his shadowy erotics of erasure and absolute control.

H.D., writing *Trilogy* during the continuously threatening years of WWII, chose a more mystical accounting of the female spirit in history, while elaborating on its multiple embodiments and reinstating it through a long, site-specific set of images, here excerpted:

> We have seen her
> the world over.
> Our Lady of the Goldfinch.
> Our Lady of the Candelabra.
> Our Lady of the Pomegranate.
> Our Lady of the Chair.
>
> . . .
>
> we have seen her snood
> drawn over her hair
>
> . . .
>
> we have seen her with arrow, with doves
> and heart like a valentine
> (H.D. 1973, part 29)

> She is the counter-coin-side
> of primitive terror;
> she is not-fear, she is not-war,
> but she is no symbolic figure
> (H.D. 1973, part 39)

H.D. positions herself most assertively where maternal power locates, in a fluid and many-faceted narrative that activates historically neglected female presence. Fragment for her, while partial, is *not* reduced to "lack" but is reconstructed with a survivor's urgency as a "particular" (embedded layer or aspect) within the reclaimed female text—seen *and* hidden—as in ancient script erased from papyrus each time a new message is written, yet always containing the shadowy build-up of origins/words/alphabets that thicken through time. H.D.'s novel, *Palimpsest,* names that very interleaving of plots and signs.

As H.D. recognized certain female presence in the antique world and tried to respeak it mythically, as part of an empowering writing practice, so Spero has recognized the necessary déjà vu evoked in the play of memory among ancient icons and contemporary female representations. Spero's modern icons do not avoid primitive terror; in fact, her female bodies often enact the "counter-coin-side" of H.D.'s "not-fear," "not-war." Spero has noted in a recent letter how she was struck by a similarity between the text of a 5th century B.C. Sumerian fable (used in her "Torture of Women" series, 1974–76):

> On her body he took his stand, and with his knife he split it like a flat fish into two halves, and one of these he made a covering for the heavens.

and H.D.'s ironic re-casting of myth from *Helen in Egypt* (used in Spero's "Notes on Time," 1976–79):

> . . . how she was rapt away
> by Hermes, at Zeus' command,
> how she returned to Sparta,
> how in Rhodes she was hanged
> and the cord turned into a rainbow . . .

Spero is interested in how both quotes foreground similar mythic patterns—while giving them different readings—in which a woman is first brutalized and then glorified (removed from ordinary dailiness) . . . what she calls "the two extremes of women's position." Like H.D., she chafes against a reductive, insubstantial, and single-minded representation of female existence. She wants "to record the celebratory aspects of women's lives, as well as the hellish."

While bringing her bound woman out of the shadow of pre-Christian classicism and into the harsh fight of Judeo/Christian modernity, Spero does not settle for this abysmal image to solely represent a fate of female inevitability but, like H.D., instigates multiplicity—a splayed-out "open field" of non-sequential, non-orderly narratives in which torture and cultural annihilation scripts are mixed with a repertoire of women energetically and often awkwardly and comically uncovering new plots for themselves in the middle of old chapters.

In Spero's Rome exhibit, women of varying historic and racial families enact their sexual and class roles in her recycled theatre of collage. Ebullient and powerful women run "out of control": Marlene Dietrich, in a pantsuit, walks directly toward you in the company of a Thai dancer printed in multiples to make a kind of chorus line. Above them, a woman in full drag sits on a chair, looking amused, while splay-legged females—straight "cunt shots"—confront you with the immediacy of a porno mag. Part archaeological/photo-fact and part fiction, '80s white girls jazzercise the aerobic way next to Egyptian maternal figures.

Spero's refusal of disembodied history is not an overdetermined one. The undeniable images of women tortured through historic time is a kind of warning and ballast. Her *femmes en parade* do not represent a marginal whitewash, enacting only the idealized layers of the *mille feuille*. The goal of her modern Woman is presence *and* active limbs . . . plus the unbound air of large enough arenas (walls, cupolas, sides of buildings) to shed the covert consciousness of the "male gaze" and gaze boldly back, a field large enough in which to recover and confront—even constitute—her own history.

H.D. and Spero share the formalized desire to break in on the "comfortable" and claustrophobic male/traditional construction of the female body and to include the *fallible* person, the *provisional* point-of-view as a legitimate part of female human existence as it appears and reappears in history. To use Amelia Jones' distinction, H.D. and Spero have created (and have fantasized) a world of female presence that instantiates rather than palliates loss.

At the Cassa di Risparmio, an important bank housed in the seventeenth century Palazzo Ricci in the Italian university hill town of Macerata, there is a permanent and formidable collection of modern Italian painting and sculpture. During a recent visit there, two things struck me forcibly in the context of having just seen Spero's show. The first was that among two-hundred plus works in this major collection, only one piece—a brooding, powerfully painted semi-abstract landscape, dated 1955—was by a woman, "A. Raphael (Mafai)," identified by my guide (a VIP of this art-loving bank) as Lithuanian in origin and wife of the painter, Mario Mafai, also represented in the collection. (On my return to Rome, I happened upon the review of a major retrospective just opening in Modena, featuring the work of Antonietta Raphael, there identified as one of the three central figures of the historically prestigious *Scuola Romana* [or *Scuola Cavour*], along with Sgr. Mafai.)

The second item of particular relevance was a bronze nude by the sculptor, Augusto Perez, 1973, called *Resurgit* (Resurrection) and the theft of affect loitering in the catalogue's description of this work. A woman stands with her head facing the viewer's gaze, eyes closed. Her naked body appears to be bound at various points along the torso and the outstretched arms and hands, as well as around the thighs and ankles, with thick lengths of fabric that prevent any movement of fingers or limbs. Her young, soft and sensuously modeled breasts are exposed. The "rhyme" with Spero's appropriated photo of a tied-up woman victim, most probably Jewish and found on the dead body of a Nazi, is remarkable, although not surprising.

The Italian version of the bound woman has been placed in one of the elaborately decorated rooms of the palazzo and is surrounded by luminous paintings, among them the prophetic technologies of power dreamed in color by Futurism's major painters—Ballo, Severini, Ivo, Dottori, and Fortunato. In the Futurist context of war's energizing combat mentality, she represents the captured property of the enemy, now the prized loot of the winners who are still in thralldom to that ancient belief in—and primitive fear of—unbounded female energy forcibly cut off.

In the catalogue for the show, the Perez bronze is described this way:

"Resurgit" is a stupendous reinvention of an historic theme that emerges in modern figurative sculpture, authentically revolu-

tionary. It is one of those figures which seems to come back before our eyes, expressing a passionate need to recover the past . . .
identified and individuated across the painful experiences of a creature that struggles with herself in the confused muddle of present
anxiety, amidst her journey between birth and death. (L. Carluccio,
art critic)

If, in fact, this bound woman has been resurrected by the sculptor Perez,
why is the replication of a terrifying though historically ordinary theme
described as "a stupendous reinvention"? What is new here, let alone revolutionary? What blind-folded projection is going on in the critic's rhetoric? Isn't it more the case that her "muddle of present anxiety" has been
talked away by him and co-opted by his comfortable liturgical drone of
cosmic magic?

One no longer needs a lengthy deconstruction of such gender-specific
interpretation to note the burden of essentialist cliché from which late
twentieth-century artists and writers must continuously extricate themselves. Spero and H.D. have replaced this murky repetition of formulaic
female pain and excess with a vocabulary of candid and accurate complexity, showing us that in diversity and specificity lie the escape from vague
"otherness." They have made evident a lifeline that is changing—and
changed by—its very struggle to become unbound.

Contingent circumstances:
Mina Loy > < Basil Bunting

A DIALOGUE

ML: Pig Cupid
His rosy snout
Rooting erotic garbage
("Songs," Part 1)

BB: Dally! Waste! Mock! Loll! till the chosen sloth fails,
huge gasps empty the loins shuddering chilly in
long accumulated delight's thunderstorm.
("Ode 9")

ML: These   are suspect places
("Songs," Part 1)

BB: Leave it to me. Only a savage's
lusts explode slapbang at the first touch like bombs.
("Ode 9")

ML: The skin-sack
In which a wanton duality
Packed?
All the completions of my infructuous impulses
Something the shape of a man
("Songs," Part 2)

BB: He will shrink, his manhood leave him, slough selfaware
the last skin of the flayed: despair.
("Ode 10," "Chorus of Furies")

FRAME: In the early Nineties, I received a letter from Keith Tuma and Maeera Shreiber inviting
me to contribute a short, non-scholarly piece to the Mina Loy collection they were co-
editing for The National Poetry Foundation. My mind drew a blank until I remembered that
when first reading Basil Bunting's *Odes*, I thought I'd heard something familiar in the tone
that connected me to Mina Loy's work. I went back into Loy and found what I was looking
for and decided to create a little dialogue between the two poets from some of their feisty,
confrontational lines. Written in 1996, this piece appeared in 1998 in *Mina Loy: Woman
and Poet* (Orono, Maine: National Poetry Foundation).

ML: I am the jealous store-house of the candle-ends
   That lit your adolescent learning

   •

   Behind God's eyes
   There might
   Be other lights
       ("Songs," Part 8)

BB: The Lady asked the Poet:
   Why do you wear your raincoat in the drawing room?
   He answered: Not to show
   my arse sticking out of my trousers.
                   ("Ode 12")

ML: Oh that's right
   Keep away from me   Please give me a push
   Don't let me understand you   Don't realise me
                   ("Songs," Part 12)

Reading through the Moyer Bell edition of Basil Bunting's *Collected Poems* some years ago, it struck me about a third of the way through the "First Book of Odes" section that a particularly candid sexuality and quirky musical resonance — familiar, yet not immediately trackable — played itself out between certain of Bunting's love poems and those of Mina Loy. I felt curious to pursue these imagined inclinations via a fictional dialogue — that is, to hunt down the basis of my speculation within the spoken lines of their poems. I'd barely made a note to this effect when, some pages later, I came upon "Ode 17," dedicated "To Mina Loy."

It seemed to me, even before pursuing my hunch, that Loy and Bunting shared — among modernist poets — a discretely ecstatic pleasure in the dense thicket of uneasy word/song/syntax made possible by a particular poetic practice favoring extreme condensation and repetition of sound, as well as the willingness to speak with a certain comic irony regarding the male-female dance.

They also shared their Englishness and were more than likely imprinted — in the early days of their writing apprenticeships — with such varieties of ecstatic compression as both Hopkins and Yeats had provided. Moreover, Loy and Bunting were both intensely grounded in the physical, addressing the sexual/eroticized body in frank pleasure *and* wariness. Extending from this physicality, their poetries give primacy to accurate, often intimate notation on the observed world's compelling presence. They both abhorred a too easily digested cant that often crept into the ideologically-blurred language of the political and artistic/literary movements that regularly surfaced around them.

Without much biographical information to guide me, I tried constructing a brief dialogue between them, made up of lines selected from Loy's "Songs to Joannes," and Bunting's *Odes*.* Only after constructing that imagined bit of sexually sparring conversation from existing texts, did I then hunt for historic evidence to back up my hunch. Thanks to an eventual exchange of letters and conversation in 1994 with Loy's biographer, Carolyn Burke, I found that Burke had written to Bunting in 1980 asking if he could shed any light on the Loy connection, as implied by his "Ode 17" dedication. Although he was eighty years old at the time and apparently not generally interested in much of the mail that arrived, he did perk up at the Burke/Loy challenge and wrote back to her with great enthusiasm.

In a letter to Burke dated July 3, 1980, Bunting reveals that he wrote "Ode 17" some seven years after paying Loy a visit in Paris.** If we are to accept his memory as accurate, that would have placed his visit around 1923–24, near the period when he first began to assist Ford Madox Ford with certain editing tasks at *The Transatlantic Review.* "I was enormously struck by her beauty," Bunting writes of that time, "though she was probably amused at my pretensions to poetry."

---

* The Mina Loy quotes used in the opening dialogue of this discussion are excerpted from "Songs to Joannes," *Others* 3, no. 6 (April 1917): 3–20. A later version of "Songs to Joannes" appeared in *Lunar Baedeker* (Paris: Contract, 1923) under the title "Love Songs," severely edited by Loy, omitting twenty-one of the original thirty-four sections, leaving only thirteen in print. The original text was restored in *The Last Lunar Baedeker* (Highlands, N.C.: Jargon Society, 1982).

The Basil Bunting quotes used in dialogue are excerpted from "Ode 9," "Ode 10," and "Ode 12," *The First Book of Odes* (London: Fulcrum Press, 1965). The odes—all dated 1929—appear again in Bunting's *Collected Poems* (Mt. Kisco, N.Y.: Moyer Bell Limited, 1985).

** The complete text of this letter was included in Carolyn Burke's discussion of it in "'The economy of passions': Mina Loy and Basil Bunting," *Sulfur* 43 (Fall 1998), 168–73.

To the twenty-three year old Bunting, Loy at forty-one must have seemed a thing apart, a successful poet who had arrived—more than once—whose poems he'd admired in *Lunar Baedeker*. Bunting writes of his visit to Loy: "She must have been nearly twice my age. . . . I was sorry that I had never tried to make love to her, though I expect she would have laughed at me." He goes on to explain to Burke that "Ode 17," dedicated to Loy, was a product of memory. "Nothing in it is more than metaphor," he writes, "except the description of her face which you have already noted" (letter to Burke, July 3, 1980).

In light of this letter, it is of interest to speculate on the currents of personal and melic/linguistic influence potentiated by this meeting.*** Bunting's "Ode 17" ends:

> Very likely I shall never meet her again
> or if I do, fear the latch as before.

A curiously decompressed couplet for a poet whose works—in the main—are so masterfully condensed and formally dazzling. But then, he was twenty-three when he met Loy; her dazzle as innovative poet and untouchable erotic object may have defeated any fantasy of conquest. In a letter to the author on September 13, 1994, Jim Powell sheds further light on this final couplet by pointing out that "the dry prosaic tone, a relaxation at the close, is a Horation move to create closure by the opposite of a ringing aphoristic couplet or the like." He reminds us that Horace was Bunting's great lyric master, thus Bunting's *Odes* are named in homage to Horace's.

Bunting would have known Loy's book-length poem sequence, *Love Songs* (composed some eight years before his first series of *Odes*), and surely would have found her tart and ironically w(e)ary tone toward her various lovers, a brilliant model to hold up before his own severe self-deprecation *and* developing taste for a diction of difficulty: poetic truth in language.

***For a brilliant discussion of melic craft and condensation informing the poems of both Loy and Bunting see Jim Powell, "Basil Bunting and Mina Loy," *Chicago Review* 37, no. 1 (Winter 1990): 6–25. My title phrase "Contingent circumstances" comes from Powell's essay. My thanks to Carolyn Burke for alerting me to the essay and to Jim Powell for so clearly elucidating and attributing value to this model in modernist poetics and practice.

Neither of them was interested in a prosody or diction reducible to summary; instead, once skepticism or desire declared itself, it was the poem's rhythmic codes and internal musics that delivered—finally—its meaning.

A reader does not go to Loy or Bunting to be lulled and coddled into familiar and soothing sound but may, instead, dip into almost any work of either poet and discover the harsh, unbeautiful "moment of truth," as well as its transformation into pure provocation via a quirky, elaborated phrasing. An apt example may be found in Bunting's "Ode 10, Chorus of Furies" (1929), in which he invents and packs his observations into a harsh, sibilant lyric:

> anonymous triple presence,
> memory made substance and tally of heart's rot:
> .
> envying idiocy's apathy or the stress
> of definite remorse.
> He will lapse into a halflife lest the taut force
> of the mind's eagerness
> recall those fiends or new apparitions endorse
> his excessive distress.
>   (Bunting 1926, from "Ode 10," 96)

Loy's *Love Songs* (1915–17)—preceding Bunting's *Odes* by twelve to fourteen years—challenge, lust after and spit out sounds like seductive ammunition:

> Prettily miscalculate
> Similitude
> Unnatural selection
> Breed such sons and daughters
> As shall jibber at each other
> Uninterpretable cryptonyms
> Under the moon

Give them some way of braying brassily
For caressive calling
Or to homophonous hiccoughs
Transpose the laugh . . .
(Loy 1982, Part 29, "Love Songs to Joannes," 104)

In spite of equally ferocious intellectual appetites, both Loy's and Bunting's works often foreground erotically charged/physically engaged natures, wounded or waylaid by potential partners and riven with a language of self-mockery and harsh acknowledgement aimed at dispelling the comforting conventions of love. In both poets, a satiric and skeptical watchfulness resides next to the readiness for encounter. However, while in *Love Songs* Loy remains wary, Bunting—his experience to the contrary—is often captured by romantic love and a rather familiar male version of his role in it, saved only by the extreme care with which he chooses and places words.

In his third "Ode," written in 1926 and dedicated "To Peggy Mullett," he immediately bares the soul of his ravenous appetites, just barely cloaked in oceanic metaphor, singing every step of the way to a surrender underscored with latent wariness:

I am agog for foam. Tumultuous come
with teeming sweetness to the bitter shore
tidelong unrinsed and midday parched and numb
with expectation.
(Bunting 1985, 89)

Perhaps it was this very vulnerability to passionate encounter that, in part, fueled the painstaking formal control in his writing. For it is in the fierce and willful formalizing of the poem's music that Bunting attempts to preserve himself from utter abandonment to excess.

Loy, on the other hand, while very much in control of her own measure, often chooses to free herself from others' musical models through spurning the achievement of a poetry infused with and marked by classical rules. Instead, she chooses the eccentric organization of internal sounds and rhymes. Jim Powell writes of her poem "Memory," but could just as well have been describing Loy, herself:

> She lives in the mind, which is a carnal thing, and wants corporeal nurture, wants in verse the carnality of a substantial music — impedance, weight, solidity, resistance: impedance like a burr to snag in recollection, resistance to outlast the corrosive blizzard of oblivion . . . a weight of phrase that sinks beyond the currents of ephemerality. (Powell, "B. Bunting and M. Loy," 12)

In her search for ways to mark her own path — as it diverged from the directives of other poetics around her — Loy often tried out devices unfamiliar in 1915 – 17 for indicating silence or a passage of time between one utterance and the next, preferring to wait — to indicate that period of search in which the unvoiced had a life as well. In quoted passages from "Love Songs to Joannes," Loy uses a three-character space between certain phrases instead of traditional punctuation; also, she chooses double-dash lines to separate her thought/line clusters and to indicate extended pauses/ rests between one perception and the next, instead of containing and completing her thought in traditionally established musical patterns. She may breathe or gaze off between composed reflections and, in fact, makes legitimate those half-articulated moments. Part 32 of "Love Songs to Joannes" begins with the direct declaration:

> The moon is cold
> Joannes

but in the third line is cut off abruptly in a suspended state of waiting and imminent flux:

> Where the Mediterranean . . .
> (106)

Loy's aesthetic assertion: To be *out of place,* contingent, never to remain static or held in thrall by another's personal or poetic agenda. Bunting's: To be as cunningly and brilliantly *in place* as possible, that place affording him the greatest possibility for control and complexity. Nevertheless, from seemingly opposite poles, an attraction to difficult directions—in diction and personal relations—compelled their mutual turning away from tradition's familiar phrase.

As a female "beauty," entering the twentieth century at age eighteen—1900 being the year Bunting was born—Loy's precocious alarm system guarded a tenuous yet tenaciously held autonomy always jeopardized at a young age by family members and, later, by lovers (often in the guise of authority figures) competing with her Muse (Burke 1997). A potential artist, inscribed at birth with formidable visual and linguistic gifts, she somehow understood the contingent power of every action, event, and encounter to give or to take. She grasped—significantly—the necessity of acknowledging this challenge to her inner life, the crucial identity that found itself only in the act of writing (and painting) according to inner dictates.

This fierce linguistically determined desire to "speak her mind" marks a poetic originality from which Bunting clearly sought sustenance and, perhaps, permission to engage at even bolder levels.

Lorine Niedecker: Beyond condensation

> Grandfather
> advised me:
> Learn a trade
>
> I learned
> to sit at desk
> and condense
>
> No layoff
> from this
> condensery
>
> —Niedecker, "Poet's work,"
> *From This Condensery,* 141

"Poet's work," written in the early 1960s, is a homely-seeming little poem, nine brief lines of self-commentary on a writing practice that first surfaced for Lorine Niedecker decades earlier, in 1922, with her first publication in the Ft. Atkinson, Wisconsin, high school yearbook. "Poet's work" locates two tenets central to Niedecker's poetry-making process, as developed throughout her career. The first was the on-going practice of revi-

FRAME: In 1994, Lee Bricetti, the director of Poets House in New York City, organized a series of talks by contemporary poets reading/commenting on the work of an earlier-established poet whose work had figured importantly in the speaker's writing life. It was within this context that I was invited to think out loud about Niedecker—her work and non-career. Although I had no new scholarly finds to offer, I did savor the rereading of her poems through the extraordinary efforts of my scholar colleagues and the chance that gave me to acquaint younger poets in the community with Niedecker's "condensery" and the many disturbing questions it raises.

Following several decades of misreading and non-reading of Niedecker's poetry, contemporary scholars have contributed major efforts toward rethinking her achievement, as discretely separate from earlier accounts that rarely mentioned her person or work—except as a "student"/acolyte to Louis Zukofsky. As a poet, I am immensely grateful for the new scholarship—in particular, for the rigorous labors of Jenny Penberthy, as well as that of Rachel Blau DuPlessis and Marjorie Perloff—without which I could never have written this piece.

sion, a life's work "at desk," expressed in the discipline of musical condensation—for her, a paring away of mannerist excess and learned poetic
verbiage that, given proper clarity, would reveal the radiant power of individual words minimally framed. The second tenet was her valuing of American speech, voiced in local conversational fragments she thought of as
"folk" background, often overheard, skimmed off and layered throughout
the larger body of her work.

Models for this spare and speech-slanted aesthetic had preceded
Niedecker in the work of William Carlos Williams and were even more
conclusively articulated for her by Louis Zukofsky's statement—as well as
his selection of poems for the "Objectivist" issue of *Poetry* (edited by him
in 1931)—although by 1928 she was "already questioning an imagist focus
on place and, before reading *Poetry* (1931), had written her first surrealist-
type poems."*

Zukofsky had opted, along with Williams, for "thinking with things as
they exist" with their "clear or vital particulars"; he stressed that *any* word
could be poetic if "used in the right order, with the right cadence, with a
definite aim in view" (DuPlessis 1992, 108). Rachel Blau DuPlessis makes
the further point that Pound's 1918 poetics prefigured the objectivist desire
for the "restrained, abstemious, antimoralizing image" that always bespeaks
"a desire to separate some essence of . . . poetry from packaging, poeticisms
and ornamentation." Like Pound, Zukofsky's idea of poetry was not directed at "mere pretty bits" (as he tended to characterize American poetry,
circa 1913), but rather focused on entire aspects of thought: economics,
beliefs, literary analytics, and so forth, "while always imbedded in the object, the particular detail" (DuPlessis 1992, 96–116). Zukofsky extended
Pound's wish to embrace those areas that seemed to have been actively
omitted from the poem in early twentieth century literary production.

Zukofsky's "Objectivist" issue of *Poetry* (February 1931) added further
impetus to Niedecker's expanding view of her poetic focus. Although the
natural world of lake, river, and swampland in her rural Wisconsin would
always provide exact information and sources of imagery, she was encoun-

---

* Jenny Penberthy, in letter to author, September 19, 1998. I am deeply indebted, throughout this talk, to Penberthy's close attention to the early years of Niedecker's development,
as set forth in her ground-breaking studies.

tering the need to attend inwardly to the peculiar movement of her own thought, how this response might also be located in *her* poetry. Gradually, her working method—the way in which she began to build and compress the syntax of her lines—became as compelling as did her characteristic subjects.

In "Poet's Work," Niedecker's intense demand upon herself as a worker/ writer is inflected in the folksy, small town maxims of her grandfather: "Learn a trade" and "No layoff" are resource and code, embodying the daily language one heard passed back and forth at any ordinary meal. DuPlessis has noted that Niedecker's "condensery" poetics may also be a bi-lingual pun on Pound's influential injunction in *The ABC of Reading,* that *Dichten* equals *condensare* (to make poetry is synonymous with the imperative infinitive *to concentrate / compress / condense*). Niedecker's "Poet's Work," or trade (that is, *Dichten,* with the further pun on *diction*) is boiling down, paring down in the condensery (DuPlessis 1992, 103).

It is understandable that a new reader, coming across *this* particular poem as a first introduction to Niedecker's work, might feel less than eager to read on. It is a poem she could afford to write *only* after more than thirty years of apprenticeship to her art. It is not the sort of poem that immediately dazzles—its urgency and craft barely perceptible—nor does it pull one into the celebratory flight of the heart nor the mysterious opacity of hidden language nor the thrill of syntactic gymnastics that often creates poetry converts. It is inward turning, plain, severe . . . a record of her passion for the vocation of wordsmith. Peter Quartermain has addressed this question:

> The risks she takes are quite extraordinary: her poems reject the grandiose, have not an ounce of pretense; there is not the slightest hint that what is said may *not* be what is meant. It is, as a result, easy to discount them as inconsequential, to rest satisfied with the inaccurate notion that Niedecker is a poet of quiet pleasures. Her poems are difficult to talk about, not simply because paraphrase seems impossible, but because there seems to be *no need* for any. Yet combine this with her scrupulous attention to

sound, and that complex play forces us to let go of the manic compulsion, so deeply ingrained in most readers, to zoom in on the meaning.** (Quartermain 1996, 220)

The "condensery," wherein Niedecker apprenticed herself, led her to a life's work of poems chiseled and fit together with complex artistry, pulling into this work a darkness seeping from her own constricted life, much of it spent caring for a deaf mother and aging father and working at jobs that had little to do with her extensive inner life as avid reader and practicing poet. In the untitled persona poem written in 1951, the year her mother died, she contraposes a fierce, unsentimental, tightly constricted music against a refrain of unremitting repetition — *as if* spoken by her mother.

II
What horror to awake at night
and in the dimness see the light.
    Time is white
    mosquitoes bite
I've spent my life on nothing.

The thought that stings. How are you, Nothing,
sitting around with Something's wife.
    Buzz and burn
    is all I learn
I've spent my life on nothing.

I'm pillowed and padded, pale and puffing
lifting household stuffing—
    carpets, dishes
    benches, fishes
I've spent my life in nothing.
    (Niedecker 1985a, 59)

**This comment was inserted, due to material made newly available, several years after this talk was originally presented.

Here she has woven a dailiness of limitation, marked by the obsessive end rhymes of dreary domestic tasks and social chit-chat where gender pecking orders undermine any sense of private mystery or artistic struggle. Of this scrutiny she has made an unsentimental poem articulate with the self-mocking knowledge of how she imagines her mother—and, perhaps, herself—as seen by their small town community. The speaker character-izes herself as "Nothing," sitting around *not* with "Something" (the em-powered but absent male), but with "Something's wife," her selfhood di-minished and identified *only* as a dutiful worker-bee enacting a repetitive and dull existence, underscored by the poem's immensely despairing re-frain: "I've spent my life on/on/in nothing."

Her mother's recent death has clearly tempted Niedecker to make a sudden and bitter assessment of the traditional limits and repetitions pro-grammed into the life of a typical housewife of that era. In the very asser-tion of *writing* the poem, Niedecker is repudiating this "nothing," invoking instead, for her own life, a more powerful set of meanings. In the refusal of a single-track identity—the claiming of her vision, and work, as poet—the radiant and private core of her life is retrieved.

.

In order to better understand Niedecker's forming poetics, one must read Jenny Penberthy's discussion of the impact of the journal *transition* *(1927–38)* on American writing, through its urging of a wide range of linguistic experiment, stimulating both the poetics and practice of innova-tive writing with "a steady infusion of new writings from the European and American—mainly expatriate—avant-garde" . . . and "publishing al-most all the major surrealists." In a "Proclamation," published in *transition* 16/17 (June 1929), its editor Eugene Jolas announced that the literary cre-ator had "the right to disintegrate the primal matter of words imposed on him by textbooks and dictionaries" and that he also had "the right to use words of his own fashioning and to disregard existing grammatical and syntactical laws" (Penberthy 1993, 24–26).

As Penberthy notes, although "Objectivist" writers contributed to this *transition* debate, it became clear to Zukofsky that although he was sympa-thetic, he was *un*willing to commit himself to the entire "disintegrating" route suggested by Jolas. In 1931, Zukofsky gave a talk entitled "Recencies" in which he declared that "The revolutionary word, if it must revolve, cannot escape having a reference. It is not infinite. Even infinite is a term" (25). Penberthy describes Zukofsky's increasing resistance, in his 1932 "Thanks to the Dictionary" rebuttal to Jolas, in this way: "Both within its scientifically precise dictionary definitions and on its associational margins, the unadorned word is sufficient. He frees words from narrow service to syntactical and contextual functions, allowing them to assert their own random particularity and eccentric reference" (25).

Niedecker read this document closely. But before her encounter with "Thanks," she'd sent a group of three poems to Harriet Monroe at *Poetry* (December 31, 1933). Her cover letter described her own version of a surrealist-inclining poetics:

> The one, "Progression", was written six months before Mr. Zukofsky referred me to the surrealists for correlation. I had explained the poem in this way: 1st section — simple knowing and concern for externals; 2nd section — the turn to one world farther in; 3rd section — the will to disorder, approach to dream . . . the individual talking to himself, the supreme circumstance. I had sketched my theory thus: Poetry to have greatest reason for existing must be illogical. . . . It is a system of thought replacements, the most remote, the most significant or irrational . . . an attempt at not hard clear images but absorption of these. (21)

She seemed, at this point, more interested in her own independently evolving surrealism than in the more objectivist-focused "hard clear image"—a tendency that Zukofsky did *not* share and eventually talked her out of. In any case, it is instructive to read the poem Harriet Monroe chose to publish—out of the three submitted—because it shows an early and transitional Niedecker, not as characteristically folksy, nor discrete and closely woven as the later work, but, instead, more playful in its wildly swinging connections. It is called "Promise of a Brilliant Funeral":

> Travel, said he of the broken umbrella, enervates
> the point of stop; once indoors, theology,

for want of a longer telescope, is made
of the moon-woman passing amid silk
nerve-thoughts in the blood.
(There's trouble with the moon-maker's union,
the blood-maker's union, the thought-maker's union;
but the play could be altered.)

A man strolls pale among zinnias,
life and satin sleeves renounced.
He is intent no longer on what directions herons fly
in hell, but on computing space in forty minutes,
and ascertains at the end of the path:
this going without tea holds a hope of tasting it.
(Chalk-faces going down in rows before a stage
have seen no action yet.)

Mr. Brown visits home.
His broker by telephone advises him it's night
and a plum falls on a marshmallow
and sight comes to owls.
He risks three rooms noisily for the brightest sconce.
Rome was never like this.
(The playwright dies in the draft
when ghosts laugh.)
                    (Niedecker 1985a, 4–5)

Clearly Niedecker is having great fun evading the linear path and feeling her way toward a cadence of jump-cuts that will free her poetically.
Her "condensing" is not yet focused as word-on-word construction, but
arrives as mental shifts of gear, allowing the unrehearsed moves of her
imagination to stand without interpretation or imposed seams, no slave to
a narrative logic.

A year later (February 12, 1934), in a letter to Harriet Monroe accompanying another kind of experiment—this one much more visually ori-

ented—Niedecker writes:"I should like a poem to be seen as well as read. Colors and textures of certain words appearing simultaneously with the sound of words and printed directly above or below each other" (quoted in Penberthy 1996, 27). The poem sequence she sent was called "Canvas"; Miss Monroe's response was to write the words "Utter mystification" across the top of Niedecker's letter and to return the poems. Three months later, Niedecker again submitted a three-part sequence, with this explanation: "'Three Poems' another experiment in planes of consciousness that will probably disturb you even more than it does me" (27).

Monroe promptly rejected the second three poems but Ezra Pound published all six in his issue of *Bozart-Westminster* (1935), though apparently with little enthusiasm. The acceptance took place because of the prompting of Zukofsky who was genuinely interested in Niedecker's ability to write from a discipline that eschewed the singular self or ego as the central focus of the poem. But reading Zukofsky's letter to Pound (re. Niedecker's work), one discovers a very patronizing, even belittling tone, proposing a superior and shared intimacy between the two men who could afford to distribute largesse—certainly a double message on Niedecker's behalf (27–28).

The first poem of the first poem sequence, while called "Canvas" in the earlier letter to Harriet Monroe, was given a new, double *ss* spelling— "Canvass"—in its only published appearance (from Jenny Penberthy, letter to author, October 1996).

CANVASS

Unrefractory petalbent
prognosticate
halfvent purloined
adark
vicissitudes of one-tenth
    steel-tin
bluent, specifically unjust
   cream redbronze
attempt salmon egress

masked eggs
ovoid
anodyne lament
bluegrean

> drying

smoke dent

exceptional retard
bald out
affidavit
flat grey shoulder.
carrion eats its call, waste it.
He: she knows how
for a testament to Sundays.
(quoted in Penberthy 1993, 29)

Although this poem is more characteristic of early Niedecker, it is fascinating to note the play of an almost obsessively musical ear throughout: it is as if she could not help her love of sound, needing to nail down a newly constructed visual awareness of the chemistry of single words placed next to each other, with very definite half-rhymes, slant-rhymes, and pure. Sprinkled through the vertical and horizontal spread of her lines, one hears and sees:

bent/vent/blu*ent*/la*ment*/dent/testa*ment*
or pur*loin*ed and *void* pushed up against re*tard* and *bald*
or all the sharp *t* sounds bonded with vowels: p*et*al, m*et*al,
out, affida*t,* fl*at, eat*s, *it*s, *it*

Penberthy reminds us of Zukofsky's important distinction regarding Lorine Niedecker's intentions:

> The object status of language is fundamental to Niedecker's poetics. Her experiment with language in later work such as "Lake Superior" has its origins in poems such as "Canvass." These po-

ems help to shift our understanding of the source of her aesthetics away from . . . the visual array of her island landscape—toward language. . . . (Penberthy 1992, 83)

.

In a nasty bit of critical smear, Donald Davie, in the 1987 issue of *Parnassus* (14:1), reduced the music of Niedecker's complete ouvre to "mannerisms" and "willfulness" and finished his pronouncement on her by saying:

> Lorine Niedecker was a poet who by her own testimony was liberated into significant utterance by the modernism she imbibed from Louis Zukofsky. Her ability to profit from that tutelage was limited by the distortions of her provincialism (which indeed she fought against); but without that contribution, it seems almost certain she would have remained a country rhymester of no account at all.

This style of moralistic finger-shaking and superior positioning of the all-knowing critic, combined with Niedecker's dependency upon the powerful (but self-protecting) mentorship of Zukofsky, has been enough, unfortunately, to throw some new and unsuspecting readers completely off the track. The obvious truth is that *any* beginning writer or artist of intelligence will instinctively reach out for and absorb the subtleties and stretch of particular models of excellence: it is the classic way of growing out of one's first limited exposure to almost *anything*. Yet even early on, in "Canvass," we see and hear a very unique sensibility marrying skepticism with playfulness—all hers.

This seems to be utterly lost on Davie. For his punishing term, *willfulness,* I would substitute the term, *acts of informed choice.* That Niedecker was listening carefully to her own peculiar mix of cadences and inventing a way to position them in the visual field of the page has completely eluded Davie. Isn't it more to the point that she chose—from all the issues of *Poetry*—the one that Zukofsky edited? That she responded with excitement to *his* statement of poetics *and* to the examples of others' poems he chose to illustrate this particular path of investigation? Clearly, it was a poetics that compelled her attention: she instinctively recognized and then consciously acknowledged a direction that would extend her range. But, as Marjorie Perloff has pointed out:

> Niedecker's version of *Objectivism* has a curiously caustic edge—a personal stringency that looks beyond the stylistic habits of her male counterparts to the specific problems of her own situation, problems in which gender certainly plays a role. It is in this sense that Niedecker resembles Dickinson . . . like Dickinson, she could never quite come to terms with the codes handed down to her by society . . . at best, it was an uneasy compromise. (Perloff 1986, 19)

In 1934, Niedecker imagined a reader coming to the poem "Canvass" and picking out musical sounds in the way that a viewer might stand before an abstract painting and respond to a play of pure color, arbitrarily or discretely placed. "Canvass," she wrote, is "a record of constrictions appearing before falling off to sleep at night. . . . Words float free or cohere momentarily to random meanings before shifting into fresh alignments" (Penberthy 1993, 28). Does this sound like the thoughts of a "country rhymester of no account at all"?

Ideas of abstraction, randomness, and montage were exciting young artists of Niedecker's literary milieu, and she did not remain unaffected. Her attraction to the musical and linguistic satisfactions of the condensation process resulted in a very original, often eccentric syntax and a language texture that extended the sound and formal range of American poetry even though, by the time of her later books, her focus on a purer, more direct rendering of language—its local and spoken usage—captured and dominated her attention.

This being said, we must ask ourselves as we listen to her poetic diction and study her structural techniques, why it is that we have been so seldom exposed to the vivid *range* of her work? What has been operative in the neglect of a poetic production both original and profoundly engaged with the core issues of a modernist American/Anglo poetics—issues indeed taken seriously in the work of other Objectivists George Oppen, Louis Zukofsky, Basil Bunting, Charles Reznikov, and Carl Rakosi. Why, when William Carlos Williams sent a letter to Niedecker, praising the originality of her prosodic forms, when Louis Zukofsky wrote on the dust jacket of her book, *New Goose* (1946): "I read only two modern woman poets, Moore and Niedecker" . . . and when James Laughlin published seventeen of her poems in the first issue of his literary journal, *New Directions,* does the current American poetry-reading public still barely know of her?

What is the explanation for her "missing person" status in most major anthologies and university textbooks? Why, in *The Norton Anthology of Literature by Women* (The Tradition in English) is there not a single poem by Niedecker, yet a beyond-generous selection of fifteen ditties by Dorothy Parker? DuPlessis puts it simply: "Canons are temporary, multiple and conflictual. They are always contested spaces" (DuPlessis 1992, 98).

DuPlessis and Perloff, in two brilliant and thorough investigations of this question, have made it very clear that the canon is always in the process of *re*formation and that questions of aesthetics and excellence are always determined by a handful of persons installed as editors of journals, textbooks, and anthologies. As Perloff has written:

> We should bear in mind that canonicity is almost invariably the enemy of the avant-garde. The genuinely new, the revolutionary, so history teaches us, is hardly apt to be quickly enshrined by the Academy. Accordingly, we must beware of proclamations that herald the New Dispensation. In his introduction to the new double issue of *PARNASSUS,* "a celebration of Women & Poetry" (Fall/Winter 1985), Herbert Leibowitz declares that "The most remarkable event in American poetry of the last fifteen years has been the eruption of Vesuvius: the emergence of talented women poets in unprecedented numbers," and he refers to women's poetry as "an historical movement—still unfolding—whose seismic waves have radically changed lives and the literary topography." But one wonders as to the aptness of the earthquake metaphor, given the fact that Leibowitz's two exemplary poets, Sylvia Plath and Adrienne Rich, were never less than celebrated and successful. Rich, for that matter, gets more space in the *Norton Anthology of American Literature* than any contemporary poet except Robert Lowell. Again one wonders about those seismic waves supposedly generated by

women's poetry when one reads, in the back of this same issue, the announcement of the next Spring/Summer issue that will include the poetry of twelve male poets to a single female one, unless, of course, "others" is a woman. (Perloff 1986)

The questions raised by these two scholars are disturbing, and the answers posed by them are both illuminating and uneasy in their complex and shifting priorities. But one thing that has struck me dramatically in my recent rereading of Niedecker's complete work—and much of the earlier male-dominant critical apparatus surrounding it—is how the poems keep getting misplaced, even buried, by the racket of competing bids for the final word on her *ouvre.*

In the same year (1985), we were given a "collected" Niedecker entitled *From This Condensery,* edited by Robert Bertholf and marked by often confusing and highly personal arrangements but positioned as definitive, as well as a "Selected" Niedecker entitled *The Granite Pail,* edited by Cid Corman who observed Niedecker's wishes as expressed in her original overseeing of the collection from which this selection was made. Unfortunately this version denies the reader—by what is left out—a full sense of Niedecker's darker personal and political themes, as well as neglecting to include dates of composition or publication with which to contextualize the writing of these works.

This frustrating mix of partial or author-unfriendly poem versions has produced a snort of condescension in critics such as Donald Davie who get pushed—rather predictably—into a dialectic of opposition, apparently unable to read Niedecker's poetry with anything more than a dismissive surface glibness because of being so focused on rebuttal. The actual poetry under discussion is then effectively muted while the egos of Niedecker's conservationists and critics are often substantially preserved in various inadequate stewardships and critical lashings.

But somewhere, waiting between the covers of these confusing "misattributions, omissions, transcription and documentation errors," Niedecker's poems continue to breathe and speak (Penberthy 1987). Thankfully, the recent editing work of Canadian scholar, Jenny Penberthy, is giving us a fresh look at Niedecker's *ouvre,* via an immense commitment of scholarship and critical explication. Penberthy's annotated editions of Niedecker's writings already include a never before published cache of twenty-nine early poems with introductory essay, "The New Goose Manuscript" (*West Coast Line* 7 [1992], 99); Niedecker's late poems, collected under the title *Harpsichord and Salt Fish* (Durham: Pig Press, 1991); and the large selection of letters, *Niedecker and the Correspondence with Zukofsky, 1931–1970* (Cambridge University Press, 1993). (Since the writing of this talk in 1993, the essay collection, *Lorine Niedecker:Woman and Poet,* edited by Jenny Penberthy, was published [Orono, Maine: National Poetry Foundation, 1996].) These volumes combine to bring a multiple-focused lens to a body of work that has quietly persevered in its impact upon the writing and poetics of numerous British, Canadian, and American poets since the late Sixties.

.

It is clear that Niedecker may have lived the most vivid part of her life in correspondence with writers who were as passionately engaged with the making of poetry as she was. Also, it is important to understand that she chose to live privately and modestly, not to reveal her poetic identity to those who shared her daily life. She wrote: "I live among folk who couldn't understand and it's where I want to live. I'd not like to appear a freak" (Niedecker to Ron Ellis, in Penberthy 1996, 94). That she drew strength from this decision, that her situation was preferred and kept her "honest," shows in her poems. She sought intellectual stimulation and dialogue with literary soul mates and recognition as a peer among them, but she did not seek a wider fame. This is perhaps one part of the reason that we are still engaged in recovering a readership for her work.

Barbara Guest: The location of her
(A memoir)

There were pictures in her rooms and none of them were reproductions. The first time I visited, I noticed gritty trails of oil pastel, the wash of tempera and gouache, torn edges of paper, lumps of oil paint and glue. The location of things: clues from the forming material world were everywhere evident and often framed. I wandered and looked while she made tea. Another time, at a large party in her uptown apartment, she was the beautiful blonde protagonist in the "whodunnit" mystery, walking among her guests, offering little bunches of purple grapes and slices of green apple from a silver tray. There was a sense of occasion, but constructed always with wry perspective . . . and some wisdom in reserve.

·

I am looking at the title page of Barbara Guest's early collection called *Poems,* published by Doubleday in 1962. Its occasion is the gathering of

---

FRAME: In the spring of 1994, Rosmarie Waldrop organized a festschrift at Brown University to celebrate the writing life of Barbara Guest and invited a number of poets to write and speak about her work. Guest's poetry and person had opened an entirely mysterious region of poetic language to me, very soon after my arrival in New York City in the early Sixties. I wanted to capture that rare transmission of knowledge that can happen when a brilliant and already developed writer is generous enough to share her time, curiosity, wit, and presence with a beginner. I wrote the piece in Rome (where I've lived for part of each year, since 1981) and sent it recorded on an audiotape that, I'm told, was subsequently shared at the festivities. This did not help my sense of loss at not being there in person to honor this utterly original poet. This essay was previously published in *Poetry Flash* (December 1994).

Guest's work from three earlier small press volumes entitled *The Location of Things, Archaics,* and *The Open Skies,* each of whose names conspire with the others to inscribe the mercurial engagement we now recognize, some thirty years later, as her mark, her charged entelechy: exactitude of the observed world; a longed-for pulse of history as retrieved human artifact; horizon of the page where almost anything might conjecture itself into language . . . and leave, as suddenly.

Guest's words are clues along the path that is actually a painting of that path. Her page can be dense and opaque with the brushed overlays of a fully covered canvas, but as often trusts the phrasal conviction of minimal gesture — the swift notation invited by sketchbook practice. She has always worked with language, as if from the live model, trusting the living fragment of the one-minute sketch, listening for musical associations as they emerge from grids of words caught in flight.

The space of Guest's page gets less and less full as it seeks openness and the unpredictable perch. A first body's traces may linger where the second and third are re-inscribed in shifting evidence of print and exposure. Fluctuating line lengths weight the grain of Fabriano. We are given accuracies without interpretation. Her page allows erasure and return.

.

There is a word in Italian, *distacco,* that refers to a little emotional distance that may be taken from a situation or conversation. Its meaning is recorded in the step backwards a painter makes when, having placed a mark on the canvas, she stops to observe how planes of light or color have massed and shifted as a result of that last placement of pigment. Whatever mark or brushwork may or may not follow takes its counsel from this moment of cool observation. This action and accretion, where mortal touch replaces stern inevitability, might describe the processive experience of Barbara Guest's compositions.

.

One night, I was at a big gallery opening, in the downtown Manhattan neighborhood below Houston Street, before it was marketed as Soho. It was sometime in 1964, probably in the autumn when everything again seemed thrilling and possible. Joe LeSueur, a guardian angel of sorts (and roommate to Frank O'Hara), had decided to watch out for me that evening, seeing that there were apparently no other identifiable women writers to be found in this crowded room. It was definitely a male network, with a few known women painters and lots of undefined fluff to fill the gaps. Joe, being kind, knew I was a bit dazzled and somewhat tongue-tied in the presence of so many of New York's most notable and risk-taking artists and, at some point, as if shifting gears in mid-air, he turned to me and demanded, "Have you met Barbara Guest, yet?"

When I said "No," his reply was simply, "Well, you must. She's writing important work, you know. Frank told me you must meet each other. Come on, we'll get him to introduce you." And off he charged, with me in tow, dropping bits of classified information like bread for me to follow. "They were in Europe at the same time a few years ago, you know, and even though there were piles of friends around, Barbara was the *only* one Frank could stand to be with if he wanted to take a serious walk, especially when there was some ancient statue that had to be visited by moonlight. He knew she wouldn't ruin it." This was intended as the ultimate compliment.

We plowed through what seemed like walls of sophistication—bodies snuggled, draped, and posed along each others' limbs, whispering intimacies, sipping white wine, blowing smoke toward the ceiling . . . a few getting sloshed. It all happened so fast I didn't have time to get nervous but was nevertheless conscious of the fact that I didn't know her work—only recently had I read a few poems here and there in little magazines. Barbara Guest's poetry seemed to occupy the place assigned to the poets' poet—a downtown reputation, akin to Joseph Cornell's boxes or Agnes Martin's pencilled graphs—spoken about as "difficult" and "mysterious." No one uptown (meaning the 92nd Street Y and other centers of well-established poetry) had yet suggested her work to me, during the few years I'd lived at the margins of literary culture in New York City. I wondered what we might talk about. My recent college education didn't seem to offer up much promising material in that room of witty rejoinders.

In fact, we never found Barbara on that particular night. She'd taken leave. But the anxious question of, "What will I possibly have to say?" hung in the air for years, preceding each subsequent meeting. Yet it needn't have. Guest's sensitivity and intellectual range enlivened every conversation. Instead of feeling inadequate, you went away determined to be both more adventurous and more exacting in books chosen and paintings studied.

Her curiosity extended to the lives and works of persons younger and less sophisticated. Her genuine interest in one's thoughts and fragile beginning poems provided a ground of encouragement; it was invaluable to feel that your speculations and impressions were considered seriously, no matter how awkwardly articulated. Her level of commitment to her work suggested a precedent for one's own uncertain approach to the demands of poetic language. She loved words and paint and took every possible occasion to enrich and protect that love. Her valuing of exchanged views preceded anything resembling obligation. This has never wavered.

I would like to note, particularly, Guest's generosity toward younger women aspiring to the vocation of poetry. It was the exception in the Sixties, when the word *mentor* more than often implied token male sponsorship based on dubious power relations. Her friendship was offered in dignity, assumed reciprocity of value and complementarity of interests. Organizing my papers recently, I found a note from her, sent to me soon after the gallery opening mentioned above. She writes: "I think that it is time we met each other, don't you? It seems that we must have a good deal to talk about."

Guest continues to provide a model for those of us engaged in finding full parity for women in the reading/writing community, beyond token representation.

·

One of my first memories of Barbara is hearing her read the poem "Parachutes, My Love, Could Carry Us Higher," on a program of New York School poets presented at the Tibor de Nagy gallery late in 1964. It was, for me, the beginning of a new plane of ecstatic response to poetic language. What was it about that poem that captured people with its labdanum resins? It was, I think, the precariousness of emotional suspension and the suggestion of imminent shattering . . . the condition of the tenuous, spoken out of a peculiarly interior experience, yet as far afield as one could imagine from the battering "confessional" model much favored in certain East Coast poetry circles at that time. Equally intriguing was the lure, eccentricity, and immediacy of that title, "Parachutes, My Love, Could Carry Us Higher," which appears twice again, threading its magical assertion through the poem as wistful proposition for radical change of direction in a psychic equation. The poem admits to doubt, midway:

> Now the suspension, you say,
> Is exquisite. I do not know.

and ends:

> yet I am no nearer
> Air than water. I am closer to you
> Than land and I am in a stranger ocean
> Than I wished.
> (*Selected Poems* 1995, 16)

The poet is not interested in one-dimensional revelation but in capturing this particular structure of difficulty. She refuses to simplify or be simplified by another's conviction or persuasion, even when it is kindly offered. The speaker's hold on language is at stake: Guest's location of self is disclosed as structural. It is in this uneasy moment that her reader is allowed entry. A recognition takes place. The perception that certainty is contextual, that *un*certainty exists as an authentic condition, hovers in relief.

·

Reading toward this celebration of Barbara Guest, I have once again been struck by the unique and extensive linguistic gifts she has brought to American poetry, reimagining its borders with both visual and comic inventiveness and the intense musical pleasure derived from her brilliantly recombinant ear. There are two of her works to which I wish, particularly, to draw your attention on this occasion.

The first, the poetic novel *Seeking Air* (published first by Black Sparrow in 1978 and reprinted by Sun & Moon in 1997), is to my mind a totally underread and thus underappreciated masterpiece of collaged plot and historic intrigue crossed with the playful banality of forgotten lists, retrieved conversations, theater of the kitchen, and the bedroom absurd.

Her black and white photographs of psychic states arise, as if from developing fluid, to gradually depict intense inner struggles of characters who compel you to live in their imagined worlds as they grope toward relation and survival. The writing, although mostly presented on the page as prose narrative, is unparalled in its lyric gorgeousness and inventive architecture.

The second work, *The Türler Losses,* was originally published as a chapbook length poem-of-parts in 1979, in Montreal's Mansfield Book Mart Monograph Series and later appeared in Guest's larger collection, *Fair Realism.* The poem turns, in part, on the purchase and loss—not once, but twice—of two fine Swiss watches (both Türlers) that disappear almost as quickly as they materialize. In a series of subtractions and substitutions, the poet's desire for the unattainable object is heightened, mocked and traced as if magnified beneath the watchmaker's lens.

Guest introduces the presence of the physical world with the literal song of a nighthawk—"Peen t Pee n t"

and, soon after, registers this passage:

> The sun dropped its leaf like a sun diary
> turning its page to shadow where the body lay
> in the shrubbery. The body moved, but with a stilly
> notion the way a wave curls over its birthday
> where nothing remains except the foam streamers,
> like giggles after deep laughter, like death closing in.
> (Guest 1995, "The Türler Losses," 95)

A gravity charges the poem's music. Naming the world's giddy and mysterious body attaches us to it, gives *it* the power to leave us. As she writes:

> Wrist watches surround themselves with danger.
> Signs. Worn clasps. Their time flies, stops.
> (Guest 1995, 95)

The Türler becomes the object around which the rest of the world is organized and understood. It mocks our belief in solidity, our half ashamed delight in ritual's expensive trinkets. Exactly at twelve noon we must begin to give up simple light, to notice the presence of shadow. We have no choice. We etch our bodies, our horses' bodies, on vases . . . hoping to survive. We say "Just a minute!" and "Later." Assuming time.

"The Türler Losses" is Guest's "Ode on a Grecian Urn"—her witness and enactment of archaic pulse beating in modern wrist, where the form of a timepiece may change but the unconditionality of loss remains the central tragic fact. I can't think of anyone who so conveys the deep sigh of the almost gone:

> All that summery wristband of blue and yellow
> faded from folds of rain like the skin beside your eyes
> where one overhears voices pacing their acres in the archery mud.
> (Guest 1979, unpaged)

Without a net: Finding one's balance along the perilous wire of the new

Part I: A cautionary tale, enacted by "the woman poet/editor," "the translator/critic" (known from this point on as "the critic"), "the young woman poet," and her husband, "the poet."

Several weeks ago, I was seated next to a critic whose work and career I had long admired. Our meeting came the day after a poetry performance given by a South American woman, whose new book the critic had co-translated from Spanish. The critic had supplied the English language side of the event and some of us who knew the poet had enjoyed a glass of wine together with them after the reading.

This friendly event had served to reinforce my supposition that the critic and I shared a certain contemporary view of literature that might reasonably include a knowledge and appreciation of the extraordinary explosion of highly innovative, non-traditional writing going on in the

---

FRAME: In 1992, the modernist scholar Gwen Raaberg put together a panel for the MLA conference in New York City on the topic of "Contemporary Woman Experimental Writers." She asked Johanna Drucker, Rachel Blau DuPlessis, and myself to discuss anything that struck us as relevant, but due to a very heavy teaching load I was having difficulty finding my point-of-entry, let alone time to write my talk. In early December, however, the perfect piece of theatre presented itself at a "literary lunch," and I appropriated the tableau as a fitting way of marking our subject. I remember, also, that nearby our MLA-designated hotel, the historic Matisse retrospective was bounding off the walls, which, in addition to all the fine scholars and poets encountered, made this particular end-of-year event unusually radiant.

Americas over the last thirty years, particularly among women writers of poetry and non-specific prose. The critic had grown up in the late Sixties and Seventies, witness to and participant in a developing consciousness in the literary community regarding, among other things, the token woman syndrome and the erasure of major modernist/experimentalist women writers from university textbooks, anthologies, and curricula.

Upon his discovery of a friendship between myself—the woman poet/editor—and a younger woman poet who was my teaching colleague, but not present, the critic broached the possibility of a meeting among the three of us during the next day-and-a-half before his departure. He had just read the younger poet's book the week before and had greatly admired it.

A lunch was arranged, in spite of it being the harried end-of-semester period for myself and my colleague-friend; we wanted to accommodate our visitor's interest. She arrived at the restaurant with her husband (a poet in his mid-thirties, also eager to meet the critic), and their energetic and verbally precocious three-year-old child in tow, for lack of a sitter. It is in this way that the woman poet/editor, the younger woman poet and her husband, also a poet, came to be eating Caesar salads together instead of grading papers *and* that the husband-poet, having positioned himself directly across from our guest of honor, was now engaging him in serious literary discussion. The young woman poet, meanwhile, was trying to listen to their discussion with one ear cocked while at the same time providing companionship for the child, at work drawing the letters of his name on the paper tablecloth.

Somewhere between dessert and coffee the poet-father took his son to the bathroom. At that point the critic turned to the younger woman poet and myself and began to comment and speculate on the situation of contemporary women writers currently working in the new formal structures often publicly referred to as post-modern, experimental, exploratory, or innovative. In this context, he brought up the subject of *HOW(ever)*, a journal I'd edited with the help of other women poet/scholars for the past eight years and that the younger woman poet had helped to co-edit during its final volume. We'd both discovered a commitment to the recovery of modernist texts by women as a part of our survival as writers.

Alas, the scholar paused only long enough to express his unhappiness with *HOW*(*ever*)'s modest number of pages and its quarterly appearance. "A journal must be of a substantial size in order to make any real impact," he complained, oblivious to this particular journal's effect within the writing and scholarly communities, despite its modest size. Nor could he calculate the economics of editing time in the lives of editor-poet-mothers who were, at the same time, employed as full-time university professors.

"Oh come on," the critic scolded, lightly dismissing our description of editing by moonlight. "I know how much time it takes. *I've* been an editor." Then he turned to the younger woman poet and asked which new women writers she was reading and learning from.

"It's hard for me to read *anyone* right now," she said — referring, at least in part, to being overwhelmed by the reading requirements of her current semester's four-course teaching load. "But I guess . . . ," and she tentatively began with a name.

"I know what you mean," he rushed in, as if her words had signaled the beginning and end of her reading list. "I can't think of *any* women writers that seem of real importance since *The New American Poetry* anthology in the Sixties." Then, registering some slight warning buzz, he looked sideways at me — the older woman poet-editor — and mumbled "Well, you know, there are a few I like . . . but I'm talking about really *significant* writing."

"Which work by women poets did you like best in that anthology?" I asked in a neutral tone, trying not to sound sarcastic, wondering which of the four in Donald Allen's 1960 collection of forty-four poets would now be cited. The critic tried to recall "exactly who was in it." I waited, curious to see which of the four women might have remained important to him. Not surprisingly, the name of Denise Levertov was the only one that he could recall. I waited a few more beats and then supplied the name of Barbara Guest. He concurred, *almost* as if he'd read her, scanning his mind for the other two. The "others" — in this case, Helen Adam and Madeline Gleason — had long since drifted from popular memory.

But the critic quickly recovered, turning to the younger woman poet. "I really like your new book," he told her. "I think that the important poetry being written now is by women in their twenties, women with first books . . . such as yours. It seems to me," he continued, "that those of you in your twenties have clearly learned from the women poets preceding you . . . and only *now* are the really interesting books being written."

"What books are you thinking of?" the younger woman poet—actually in her mid-thirties—asked quietly. The critic mentioned a particular name with great enthusiasm and then tried to think of others while we patiently ate our salads.

Part II: Commentary

One might imagine the effect of being *either* of the women poets at that lunch: to be erased in one perfunctory sentence *or* rewarded, that swiftly . . . having published one book or having published many. Becoming part of the literary record of one's time or not—tokenized *or* dismissed with such unquestioning certainty, such unconscious ignorance. What impact does this have on any person's ability to work, to keep pushing the limits of one's art, walking the perilous wire of the new, as arrows and roses descend haphazardly from the same, small, barely visible judging booth year after year.

It is partly the immediate physical impact of this particular critic's tone of voice, his presumption of superior and indisputable insider knowledge, his self-assured right to pronounce such sweeping and final-sounding judgments on what is actually an immense and discretely particular body of innovative work achieved by women since that 1960 Allen anthology— work still very much in-process, work to which the visitor, apparently, had allowed himself little exposure.

It is not so much the small bruise of this particular encounter, but rather what the critic's voice chillingly represents—a system of selection and reward that has been passed around among inherited networks, seemingly off-hand decisions made over Caesar salads, casual but binding agreements about what is pleasing and relevant for publication—aesthetic tastes and refinements rooted historically in a kind of pow-wow model only recently persuaded of its ethical responsibility to include certain token "others." In this male economy, the official avant garde has at least been assigned a contemporary representative, persuaded by its predominating scholars that John Ashbery is a poet to be read seriously. But apparently, some-thing still remains troubling about women writers—even feminists, god forbid—working outside the tradition of the personal lyric or the classical epic forms.

Whose status quo does it threaten?

Part III: Analytica femina

Waking up inside this literary sociology early in the Seventies, with Simone de Beauvoir tucked in pocket, the tradition-resistant woman writer—who may not yet realize she is becoming one—begins to question the existing conditions of publishing. By the mid-Seventies she is quite clear that the more interested she is in pushing the structural and musical limits of the poem, the less welcome her work is in the essentially male-edited main-stream magazines. Still, she needs a readership, a community of conversa-tion. Turning to the cooler rhetoric of a male-edited avant-garde, in its various Sixties and Seventies incarnations, does not pose a promising alter-native at this particular moment since she is yet unable to articulate a fixed aesthetic position. She doesn't know precisely, from one poem to the next, what she's up to, whereas the visible experimentalist literary journals seem to know exactly what is and isn't worthy of their attention.

Women-edited publications emerging in this period of the early Sev-enties would—one assumed—appear to be more receptive to the asser-tion of uncertainty and multiplicity in female experience and its tenuous extension into language. In France, Luce Irigaray and Julia Kristeva were already exploring this difference theoretically. If men had historically owned the territory and dictated the aesthetic terms, one hoped that female edi-tors would be available in a less rigid way to support the idiosyncratic originality of contemporary writing by women.

However, while a ground swell of women's writing and publishing sur-faced in the Seventies and Eighties, much of it adopted a single-voice identity model for exploring gender issues and sexual love. Ranks ap-peared to close, rather than open, as the powerful ideology of a "common language" took hold and became the central tenet of a feminist poetics. That the received structures of inherited language—so deeply embedded at the levels of genre, grammar, lexicon, and syntax—might be critiqued, struggled with, mocked, or reconstructed in the very activity and body of the poem's making seemed to pose a threat. It was as if there were no tolerance for the contemporary extension of that "new music" inherited from Dickinson and further pioneered by the brave and highly imagined writings of the modernist women preceding us.

Nevertheless, in a world of Marie Curie, particle physics, John Cage, Twyla Tharp, Marxist dialectical models, Helen Frankenthaler and Louise Nevelson—not to mention the confrontation of Freud and Lacan by French women psychoanalytic thinkers—there were, by the mid-Seventies, other models for thinking about female experience as represented in writing. The effort to linguistically construct a feminine subjectivity had once again begun.

Slowly, news of the modernist women experimentalists began to surface. Until this time, it was as if we'd slept in ignorance, our links to these enlivening sources unavailable. This erasure of information only served to reinforce the comfortable myth of a limited poetics practiced by women, confined to the safe hearth of the personal/autobiographical lyric. Stein and Barnes, Richardson, Loy, and Niedecker might earlier have provided women writers with any number of possible experimental models, had their works been available.

Because the modernist project we'd inherited did not include the off-beat, risk-taking texts of many of modernism's principle female players, we were denied access to their interiority and the fragmented, dislocating language invented to map it. Women who were attracted to these new sounds and unfamiliar structures had only the male half of their family— thus far—to provide them with forms of experiment and critique.

But lest you too quickly characterize "the censor" as having only one gender or imagine that things can never roll backwards to an old mentality, let me assure you that the current publishing story has not been without blemish. In 1985, a Bible-size debut, *The Norton Anthology of Literature by Women: The Tradition in English,* arrived in hundreds of university mailboxes of teachers of English literature and Women's Studies. Its title was emblematic: it pitched itself as *the* tradition, as if there were but one unchanging truth about writing.

Reviewing its table of contents, the first thing that struck me was that although Dorothy Parker was represented by fourteen entries of witty light verse in the section called "Modernist Literature," Dorothy Richardson's brilliant, twelve-volume poetic novel *Pilgrimage* was assigned a two page sample (preceded by a two page historical note). Furthermore, no mention was made of Mina Loy, Laura Riding, Mary Butts, Ivy Compton Burnett, Lola Ridge, or Genevieve Taggart.

In the section designated "Contemporary," an ample selection of mainstream Afro-American women was registered, while Ntozake Shange— whose idiosyncratic pile-up of phrase/upon/phrase attempts something structurally close to be-bop (her music marked with up-ended/Dickinson-like slashes)—was not there, nor were the works of Jane Bowles, Evelyn Scott, Lorine Niedecker, Daisy Alden, and Barbara Guest—all publishing actively in the Forties, Fifties, and/or Sixties. Not registered. From sea to shining sea.

Perhaps, the most conspicuous absence of all—because it is so total— was the erasure of on-going and recent experiment in poetry and prose. In 711 pages of contemporary writing by women, not a single representation of current innovative practice is in evidence, no reference to the more than 100 women writing and publishing in English, radically opening up the terrain of contemporary literature since the late Sixties. It must be noted that at least half of these living writers had published three to five books by the time the Norton Women's anthology was being assembled.

The message: don't wait around to be discovered. Get to work and make your own. Billie Holiday said it best.

Part IV: Action's elixir

A major change, however, is in-the-making. In recent years, there has been an increasing flurry of publishing activity initiated by women writers turned editors. Due to a network that came into existence during the years of editing *HOW*(*ever*), these journals now arrive regularly in my mail. Among those engaged with new writing, many are women-edited and focus on poems of syntactical dislocation, complications of grammar, and shifting lines of subject demarcation in the once stable genres asserted as "THE Tradition in English."

Dickinson understood, as did Stein, that one's linguistic perspective is inseparable from gender and that new—if traditionally uncomfortable— terms are needed with which to inscribe the at-oddness of a life whose forms of cultural expression and exclusion are continuously inherited and reforming.

Part III

Continuum . Contingency . Instability

The New comes forward in its edges in order to be itself;

its volume by necessity becomes violent and three-dimensional
and ordinary, all similar models shaken off and smudged

as if memory were an expensive thick creamy paper and every
corner turned now in partial erasure . . .

(KF, "WING," 1995)

Line. On the Line. Lining up. Lined with. Between the lines. Bottom line.

> Type headings, excerpted passages, poetry, etc., indented
> uniformly or flush left. Don't center anything.
>
> —from *Preparation of Manuscripts on Word Processors
> and Computers*, University of Illinois Press

The line, for a poet, locates the gesture of longing brought into language. It is the visual enactment of perspective and difference. Whether that point of view rests primarily in musical voiced units or invented visual clusters, the line reveals a great deal—intentionally so when it is visibly notating the moving path of a poet's discovering intelligence or unintentionally when it is merely repeating or echoing agreed upon codes of "right" music, "serious" subjects, or "well-crafted" metric constraints. A poem whose line breaks adhere to these comfortably established systems can hope for easier access to the literary community, the canon; that poem has well-programmed scanners, advocates of the known ready to recognize its virtues.

Alas, the poet whose oeuvre is essentially spent in emulating, catching-up with, and achieving a repetition of the known has got to be swallowed

---

FRAME: In the mid-Eighties, Robert Frank and Henry Sayre were putting together a collection of essays on "the line," eventually called *The Line in Postmodern Poetry* and published in 1988 by the University of Illinois Press. Marjorie Perloff gave them my name, and they contacted me. I had never written a formal essay and was untutored in the scholarly process, thus anxious about committing to such a project. When I expressed my timorousness to Perloff, she refused to take my worry seriously and assured me that I could do it. I will always be grateful for this needed push, for as I thought about it further I realized that one of the few things I felt sure I knew something about was the line—particularly as it was being reinvented by innovative women poets at that very moment. I'd thought about it in my own work for years and in the works of dozens of talented students and friends. For me it was a graphics of revelation.

by her own accommodating shadow; there is very small chance of repeating the particular brilliance of the original master's work and still remaining free to imagine her own experience in new formal terms. For the masterpiece, the poem admired and held up through time and still setting us aquiver with suspended delight, unknowing and—ah!—disturbed acknowledgment, is a poem in which its author was largely able to deny or push beyond the outside world of acceptable, over-used, blunted, and bullying language usage to attend, instead, to some dangerous and intimate region of the unsaid.

The poetic line is a primary defining place, the site of watchfulness where we discover *how* we hear ourselves take in the outside world and tell it back to ourselves. There are very few great poets who have not taken chances with the line, perceived it as a tool for reassembling language to a new order—one's own, at that moment.

For this reason, the frame of the page, the measure of the line, has provided for many contemporary women poets the difficult pleasure of reinventing the givens of poetry, imagining in visual, structural terms core states of female social and psychological experience not yet adequately tracked: hesitancy, silencing, or speechlessness, continuous disruption of time, "illogical" resistance, simultaneous perceptions and agendas, social marginality.

Emily Dickinson was, perhaps, the first woman poet to provide other women with a formal model of urgency and difference. Susan Howe has written of Dickinson that she:

> built a new poetic form from her fractured sense of being eternally on intellectual borders, where confident masculine voices buzzed an alluring and inaccessible discourse, backward through history into aboriginal anagogy. Pulling pieces of geometry, geology, alchemy, philosophy, politics, biography, biology, mythology, and philology from alien territory, a "sheltered" woman audaciously invented a new grammar, grounded in humility and hesitation. HESITATE from the Latin, meaning to stick. Stammer. To hold back in doubt, have difficulty speaking. "*He* may pause but *he* must

not hesitate."—Ruskin. Hesitation circled back and surrounded everyone in that confident age of aggressive industrial expansion and brutal empire building. Hesitation and Separation. The *Civil War* had split America in two. *He* might pause, *She* hesitated. (Howe 1985, 21)

How she hesitated, rather than *why*, is more the subject here: how Dickinson visualized that uncertainty that punctuated her daily life and thought. One sees the starting and stopping movement of doubt within her line, as well as between lines, as we watch each unit lurching forward, both separated by a dash and rushing forward through the seeming haste of that dash to the next perception or extension. The argument of parts: one Emily hesitant to say, another Emily eagerly rushing in—if stammering—with a further ironic shift of view. In this poem, she both speaks her dilemma and shows it:

> I felt a Cleaving in my Mind—
> As if my Brain had split—
> I tried to match it—Seam by Seam—
> But could not make them fit.
>
> The thought behind, I strove to join
> Unto the thought before—
> But Sequence ravelled out of Sound
> Like Balls—upon a Floor.
> (Dickinson 1960, 937)

In this seeming disclaimer, the dismayed witness, Dickinson, observes her "inadequacy" in retaining a single wholeness of vision or rational sequence of thought (clearly required of her by the world she is addressing) and, at the same time, intentionally displays it with such an exacting set of images—unraveling them with dashes as she goes—that we are pulled into her fragmenting sense of the world and recognize that knowledge of rupture as our own. It is as if she had legitimized the disturbed otherness

of a mind not in sync with the assumptions of polite society, whose masculine thought and poetry appeared as seamless events, unruptured, smoothly
in control.

Often, when students are slipping into poetry with the help of a university education, they will be taught rules of prosody from such expert guides
to English verse as John Hollander's brilliantly succinct and witty "rules of
thumb," *Rhyme's Reason*. Although Hollander makes it clear that an accomplished mastery of these rules and traditional forms does not a poem
make, this point is unfortunately often missed in the classroom. His own
originally composed examples of verse — pure accentual, pure syllabic free
verse of a dazzling variety — are formally impeccable, fun to read, and
leave one struck with admiration at the control and mastery so apparent in
his rendering. There is no hesitation showing, no evidence of ambivalence,
no disturbed stutter of a voice either unable to speak or chaotically pouring forth after being self-edited or deleted over an unbearable length of
time. One experiences Hollander's pleasure in accomplishment, not his
resistance to tradition's fond embrace. His guide embodies the authority of
historical privilege.

One may admire it and at the same time feel a sudden silence of resistance descending, if one is a woman trying to give shape to her own
experiences, yet perceiving that almost all the models being held up to her
have been created largely out of male privilege and assumed access to
public speech. The confidence that existing poem forms cover the essential and important areas of human experience is a troubling barrier to the
discovery of new formal possibilities.

.

Given this resistance, how have contemporary women poets visualized —
structurally — that marginal and unspoken region they've claimed as difference? After Emily Dickinson, modernist women writers provided the next
maps and notations. H.D. introduced the concept of the *palimpsest:* writing
layered into the before and after of other writing . . . documents that,
through time and benign or active neglect, have been imperfectly erased,
defaced, lost. In H.D.'s poetics, a particular moment in history may often
be *re*inscribed by a contemporary woman writer over the faded or dim-

ming messages of a female collective consciousness, unearthing in this process a spiritual and erotic set of valuings essentially ignored by the dominant culture.

The imaginative part of the palimpsest notion is that some of the imperfectly erased writing from ancient female texts and myths may still
come through — bits and pieces of language, single words, alphabet fragments whose traces and marks suggest the challenge of coded hermetic
messages, both from recovered past writings and from one's own word
history. It was H.D.'s now famous experience of seeing hieroglyphs hovering on the wall of her hotel room and her reading of those as gifts from her
muse — Winifred Bryher, her companion, literally seeing *and* seeing H.D.
through the final vision — that released her into a new and infinitely more
complex way of writing.

.

In current poetic practice, a number of women have found their own
quite different ways of visualizing the palimpsestic notion. The New York
poet Hannah Weiner, in her book *Clairvoyant Journal,* shows a photo of
herself on the cover with the phrase "I SEE WORDS" written across her
forehead in paint. This gesture playfully visualizes (1) a factual event of her
life, and (2) the structural solution she developed, via a poetic line crowded
with clusters of smaller line units. Weiner employed this technique for
inscribing accurately what she saw, literally, projected outward (onto walls
and other persons' foreheads, for example). She took the unique experience of clairvoyance (in this case, seeing words not visible to others and
hearing voices "from the outside"), as well as the more common experience of interior multiple "selves" or "voices" speaking and perceiving within
a single though sometimes chaotic mind, and employed precise elements
of visual typography to display these voices and projected words. (See fig.
17, p. 191.)

Weiner has clearly conveyed a picture of ruptured perception and interior static with the conscious, line-by-line placement of her material, in-
serting fragments of thought and multiple speaking voices as line units
inside of the longer line that pushes up against the furthest margins of the
page, rigidly flattened against the left margin unevenly jagged down the
right (this stagger, a function of her particular IBM typewriter's refusal to

justify its right-hand margin), which she embodies as part of the headlong rush of voices, signboard slogans, "commands" from the outside.

•

Another poetic work particularly attuned to the possibility of linear (yet non-linear) multiples suggested by the palimpsest trope is Rachel Blau DuPlessis's "Writing." This work finds some of its foreshadowing in the ideas and writings of H.D., discussed by DuPlessis in a number of her essays, among them one called "Language Acquisition" (*The Pink Guitar* 1990) in which she notes the developing speech of her small child as one ongoing contrapuntal line of observation throughout the text and interweaves "this babble, these baby melodies" with "reactivated rhythms, intonations, glossalalias . . . of the speaking subject" (Julia Kristeva, as cited by DuPlessis 1990, 253), and with H.D.'s experience of seeing light pictures on a wall.

In DuPlessis's long poem "Writing," this back-and-forth of early sounds, small cries, explicit fragments of speech being actively pressed into the world by the infant, becomes part of the altered consciousness of the adult—the woman/mother/poet who is suddenly hearing meaning in single syllables and is attempting to notate these primary sounds and meanings, layering them with her own complex residue of mundane domestic details broken by ecstatic moments of "vision" or intellectual perception (fig. 3).

The poetic line is seen to struggle, running little columns of half-words or crowded rushes of sound or syllables splitting to reveal multiple readings. Next to these typeset words there is sometimes a concurrent voice, inscribed by hand in dark ink that leaves its traces in and around the first text, protecting *and* speaking with it (as a mother might utter little bits of talk to an infant while holding it), allowing the mark of more than one voice or self to be present—the seen reality of the fragmented, simultaneous moods of the maternal experience so common among women, yet unlocated in poetry until contemporary women poets could first acknowledge its absence and then find ways of bringing it onto the blank page.

In her "Working Notes," which accompanied the initial publication of this excerpt, DuPlessis describes the intention of her project: "Writing from the center, the centers of, otherness . . . understanding formal marginality. Marginalization. Setting the poem so there is a bringing of

SoMANy DISTANCES INTO INVENTION
. sing way-   *A TREK. ACRoss SLUGGISH*
ward black   *END-WINTER GRASSES, DARK SCRAPS*
against grey brown against *TWIG BLOWN, LIMB DOWN A ROT*
black gave small
twig   *AND FEATHER-WHITE WOOD*
s un stinting.

                  ALL SCRABBLE AND GROUND
Without silver
remarks without glistening   *UNITCHED VERY ITCHY*
tone the little feeling touch   (imbeddings, angles)
light as it is   *BUT SUCH A BIG AREA, SO MANY*
what is that   *LEAVES*
the .   *AND THEY BLOW*
                  THEY BLOW
                  THEY BLOW.

Fig. 3. From Rachel Blau DuPlessis, "Writing," *HOW(ever)* 2, no. 3 (1985)

marginalization into writing. Putting that debate right in the piece by making several sayings or statements be in the same page space...." (DuPlessis 1985, 1).

                              •

In contrast to having so much to say that it is bubbling up, crowding and urgent in its pressure on the line, there is the discrete, wary, measuring eye of Lorine Niedecker, often spoken of as "the only woman in the Objectivist movement" or "Louis Zukofsky's protégé," yet not included in the "Objectivist" issue of *Poetry* (Feb. 1931) or in *An "Objectivist" Anthology* (1932), because—as Carl Rakosi remembers it—"her manuscript didn't arrive on time" (from a conversation with the author in 1983).

Largely due to the efforts of Cid Corman, editor of *Origin,* we have her letters and poems and can attend to the tenacious, sinewy poetic line she developed, which leaves out everything except the most tested (and trusted) utterance. There is more silence in her poems, perhaps even more unsaid between the lines, than in Emily Dickinson, from whom she must have learned as a kindred spirit across time.

Niedecker sometimes seems to float her bare yet delicate unrhymed tercets as if on air; other phrase clusters are lined-up with the precision and rectitude of the orb-weaver spider. The effect is almost lace-like, yet bears the weight of enormous pressure: "economies undertaken for the joy of seeing how much a few words will bear" (Dahlen 1984).

> The eye
> of the leaf
> into leaf
> and all parts
> spine
> into spine
> (Niedecker 1968, from "Traces of Living Things," unpaged)

In 1965, Niedecker wrote Cid Corman "that meaning has something to do with song—one hesitates a bit longer with some words in some lines for the thought or the vision—but I'd say mostly, of course, cadence, measure make song. And a kind of shine (or sombre tone) that is of the same intensity throughout the poem. And the thing moves. But as in all poems, everywhere, depth of emotion condensed . . ." (Niedecker 1986, 64).

> Nobody, nothing
> ever gave me
> greater thing
>
> than time
> unless light
> and silence
> which if intense
> makes sound
> (Niedecker 1968, from "Wintergreen Ridge," unpaged)

Beverly Dahlen observes that Niedecker's "light . . . became by some synesthetic process the 'tone,' that light perceived as sound. Yet tone is more than sound, always difficult to hear or name. It's what is there inside the sound, the song or given measure; it has to do with the substance of the poem, its concrete particular thingness. But not static. The 'intensity' she says, that pressure under which the (thing? poem?) turns, is transformed" (Dahlen 1984).

As in Dickinson's poems, pressure and condensation become both tool and measure for elucidating briefest moments of discovered truth. This "condensery" was all that Niedecker—in person, very shy and private— could afford; anything more would have been for her untrustworthy verbiage, romantic dissembling, frills of popular song language.

•

Susan Howe, sharing Dickinson's puritan rigor of attention and Niedecker's trust of condensation, brings further pressure to bear upon individual words and parts of words. Her love of sound is always located in her impassioned reclaiming of an historic female perspective through a reinscribing of the voiced thoughts of women erased or effaced through disregard or partial understanding—voices such as Mary Rowlandson (author of a "lost" captivity narrative), Stella (Jonathan Swift's unusual woman friend), and Cordelia (daughter of Shakespeare's *King Lear*). The echoes and startled syllabics emitted from these voices of the past are embedded in Howe's own painstakingly composed lyric structures (fig. 4).

•

In this passage, Howe lines up double columns of language that push and pull, question and mock the status quo of traditional, left-margin ordering of verse and logic, cramming each line with sound that crackles and yaws with the plosives and hissings of a lowercase heroine—demeaned, tiny, common, ridiculous—in contrast to the uppercase Hero men. (Heroine's line is half the size of Hero's . . . and heroine mocks herself, her appearance of acquiescence to the well-scanned plot, in her comment "only nonsense/my bleeding foot").

In countless other examples, Howe takes a whole page as a canvas (she began as a painter) and positions words as in a field—a minefield or mind field—in which the line does not present itself as continuous flow but pinpoints, frames or locates one vulnerable word at a time for its own resonance, time value, visual texture, and meaning—apart from its connection to what precedes and follows it. She insists on slowing down both her perception and the reader's. She leads us into paying attention to both

WHITE FOOLSCAP

Book of Cordelia

heroine in ass-skin
mouthing O Helpful
= father revivified waking when
nickname Hero men take pity spittle speak

only nonsense
my bleeding foot
I am maria wainscotted
cap o'rushes tatter-coat
common as sal salt sally
S (golden) no huge a tiny
bellowing augury

NEMESIS singing from cask
turnspit scullion the apples pick them Transformation
wax forehead ash
shoe fits monkey-face oh hmm
It grows dark The shoe fits She stays a long something
Lent is where she lives shalbe shalbe
loving like salt (value of salt)

Fig. 4. From "White Foolscap: Book of Cordelia," *The Liberties,* in Susan Howe, *Defenestration of Prague* (New York: Kulchur Foundation, 1983), 86.

the fragility and the strength of each word she has recovered and un-clothed of its assumed historic habits. She asks what is gloss and what is babble; what does it mean for women poets to go beyond traditional ideas of "serious" and "well-crafted" verse? How are we undone, slighted by traditional constraints and what is left in the ensuing silence?

·

A painterly affection for light, color, formal relationships of line to space combined with analytical attention to these qualities, through the medium of language, marks a family resemblance inside the larger family of women poets practicing within the bounds of the modernist sensibility. Certainly, Howe's visual concerns reflect a shared perspective with Barbara Guest and, earlier, with Mina Loy. Loy, a serious painter as well as poet, spent time in the company of Italian futurist and French cubist/surrealist artists and writers; Guest began her career as a primary figure in the New York School circle, writing often about painters and painting, even as she developed her own poetic compositions, collaborating with several women painters on word/painting experiments.

Among Guest's many books, perhaps the most stunningly inventive poetic work is the novel, *Seeking Air,* in which Guest views the overall plot as a kind of disrupted text—erasing actions, overlaying characters' thoughts like bits of fine-colored tissue used in collage, intruding upon the narrative with a science report, a list found in a pocket, a page torn from *The Listener* book review section, a recipe, quoted passages from such writers as Jonathan Swift and Chiang Yee—all juxtaposed with mysterious small narrative chapters resembling cubist prose poems.

In the page reproduced from *Seeking Air* (fig. 5), one sees a kind of canvas on which is placed a delicate grid of words—her construction of the line as visualized word-by-word—the floatingness of the poetic language grounded below with a paragraph of on-going prose "explanation." Honor Johnson writes that Guest has always sought "techniques of abstraction and methods of composition that might be applied to words and their reinvented relations inside the poem. . . . [She] writes in the company of Stein, in her non-linear shifting from line to line, but she is less interested in pinning down a single situation or person. Whereas much of Stein's work is pushed forward by syntax and has a compulsive drive which gives it power and rhythm, Guest argues for a kind of poem that opens out into vistas or perceptual lyric spaces" (Johnson 1984, 12).

The benign critical neglect of Guest's work in the Seventies repeats the dilemma of the majority of women modernists often discussed, as Carolyn Burke so aptly points out, as "isolated cases." Burke suggests that it may

82

Lustrous Polychromes

Cypress, eucalyptus, magnolia, oak, olive, palm, sycamore, orange, lemon, jacaranda, pine, yucca

Bougainvillea, gardenia, geranium, camellia, rose, oleander, succulent, begonia, sage, thyme, heather, pansy, pink

Fog.   Sun.   Heat.   Coolness.

Mountain.   Sea.   Canyon.   Desert.

Dry.   Parched.   Green.   Watered.

Smudge pots.   Acqueducts.

Porch.   Balcony.   Grill.   Gates.   Hedge.   Stucco.
Tile.   Wall.

Deep shadow.   Ardent light.

Somewhere beneath this radiance there ran still a turbulent current which erupted in my dreams. Fresh landscapes would appear and on them posed portraits of my friends, often in threatening attitudes. Animosities and ambivalences advanced and retreated and morning found me gathering sums of paranoia. This unpleasantness fitted so ill into the scenes of my waking life composed of friendly cats and dogs, mourning doves and the activities of the natives vigorously commuting from mountain to beach, driving their campers and charming miniature cars, the illusion of health, if not happiness everywhere.

Fig. 5. From Barbara Guest, *Seeking Air. A Novel* (Santa Barbara: Black Sparrow Press, 1978; reprint, Los Angeles: Sun & Moon, 1997).

also testify to a slight discomfort with women who do not assert the self in writing, who instead write in part to bring into question the very notion of the self (Burke 1985).

.

What can an accurate skeletal picture reveal about the subject? Or, if the subject is yet to be brought into focus, what learned prohibitions have women poets worked against to uncover and catch partial knowledge, fragmentary perception that disappears almost as fast as it arrives? What if the subject, itself, is resistance, vulnerability, seeming lack of will, the conditioned self-denial that creates uncertainty, unsteadiness in the world? How can the line be made to reflect these states?

In Frances Jaffer's poem "The flame the," she begins with the word *refusal;* her first line—"refusal the"—continues the title's fragmentary lurch and is intentionally unpretty, with no immediately containable referent. She is trying to catch her own hiding, some antisocial resistance, part of a dialogic puzzle trying to work itself out inside her. This sarcastic private remark she's just heard in her mind is now speaking out to an "other," yet still camouflaged within the text of the poem:

> *The flame the*
>
> refusal the
> Umbilicus we whip with? All that
>
> fidelity stuck to a scope
>   I rage you
>   rage we rage aren't we
> together though
>   and the warm water how
>
>   and the sweet cool
>   morning
>   (Jaffer 1985, 25)

Jaffer mocks her seeming self-satisfaction ("aren't we / together though") by the way she breaks her line so that it doesn't end in a traditionally predictable way, while yet allowing, in a condensed shift, another fragment (and tone) to float to the top—"and the warm water how"—suggesting an undervoice or palimpsest echo of spiritual healing. In this case, line length manages the flow of the timing in the poem and in the poet, as well, who insists on giving herself permission to wait, to resist closure, to allow some other partial voice in her psyche to have its awakening and its say.

·

Resistance is an ongoing condition-of-being for most women poets . . . the inability to say how it is or not wanting to say, because what *wants* to be said and who wants saying can't be expressed with appropriate tonal or spatial complexity in the confident firm assertions cheered on by witty end-rhymes or taut lines marching with left-margin precision down the page. What wants to be said is both other and of "the other world." It wants words and worlds to be registered in their multiple perspectives, not simply *his* or *yours.*

·

The stress inflicted by the inability to say, to have a say, to speak, to come upon silence instead of desired utterance, to understand finally one's deepest mistrust of language, underlies or interleaves the text of Beverly Dahlen's work, which often buries its discrete line units inside a "sentence" or "paragraph." But these visual conventions belie their first impression and are often undone by the notation of uncertain time or scrabbled memory within unconventionally punctuated units. One interesting revision and remaking of an entry in her long work, *A Reading 1-7,* may reveal a "truer" version of the original story.

Dahlen first presents a kind of journal entry or letter form, whose visual presentation is that of a paragraph, even though its internal clauses stop and start, fitfully, with the help of uneasy punctuation:

> Dear Rachel, about aphasia you're right, but she was she and really had it, unlike Mark who first suggested it years ago as an idea about poetry, how it is written anyway. of course it was right for

me, stutterer, silent child. one day I would meet a real one, some
other the wind blew through. she was tattered. a presence.

I would not have been a poet for all these reasons because I was
indecisive. now I know. I could not drag it in. dragging it. the
drowned mermaid. why, in her own element. it was not my element. neither air nor water. here they say one becomes acclimated.
learning how to live in an artificial environment. it is called California but I'm not sure.

(Dahlen 1985, 78)

Across from these "paragraphs" is a second version of the original:

San Francisco
March 5–April 20, 1979
Dear Rachel, about aphasia you're right, but she was she and really
            Roman Jakobson
had it, unlike Mark who first suggested it years ago as an idea
        language,   forgotten   this theory, this disease as metaphor
about poetry, how it is written anyway. of course it was right
        stutterer
for me   child. one day I would meet a real one, some
        silent
                            contiguity disorder
other the wind blew through. she was tattered. a presence.

I would not have been a poet for all those reasons because I was
inconsolable

        . now I know. I could not drag it in. dragging it.
indecisive.
the drowned mermaid. why, in her own element. it was not my
element. neither air nor water. here they say one becomes
acclimated. learning how to live in an artificial environment.

it is called California but I'm not sure.

(Dahlen 1985, 79)

Dahlen tries to visualize through a kind of floating line and a palimpsest overlay or insertion of new material (as well as displacement of original material) a more accurate picture of the relationships of her thought, memory and current reading. In this second version, perhaps looking to our habituated eyes more like a poem, the poet displaces and brings new attention to painful words: stutter/silent/inconsolable/indecisive. She interlines additional and tension-producing language: Roman Jakobson/forgotten/this theory, this disease as metaphor/contiguity disorder. . . . She makes for herself (and, perhaps, for her reader—in this case, Rachel) a clearer suggestion of how the poet hears or sees things simultaneously, momentarily. She does not want to force these floating, telegraphed bits of language into a tidy blueprint, an impenetrable house of bricks, but rather to allow the material of her constructed experience to be available to different readings, for her own elucidation as well as the reader's.

.

Breaking rules, breaking boundaries, crossing over, going where you've been told not to go has increasingly figured in the writing of the contemporary woman poet as a natural consequence of the restraints placed upon her as a child being socialized to the female role her class and culture prefer. The poem becomes her place to break rank: *her* words, *her* line lengths and placements, *her* "stuff." Ntozake Shange, in the poem "Somebody ran away with all my stuff," makes her claim by inventing a way to pile up the "stuff" of her lines. Spoken as a monologue in the play *for colored girls who've considered suicide, when the rainbow is enuf*—several years after its first version as a poem—this writing is a rant and rave, a saxophone solo, an insistent demand to be left alone and allowed to have her own life with all its idiosyncratic desires, its ambivalent attitudes, its this *and* that, on her own terms, in her own vernaculars:

> hey man/ where are you goin wid alla my stuff/
> this is a woman's trip & i need my stuff /
> to ohh & ahh abt/ daddy/ i gotta mainline number

from my own shit/ now wontchu put me back/ & let
me play this duet/ wit this silver ring in my nose/
honest to god/ somebody almost run off wit alla my stuff/
& i didnt bring anythin but the kick & sway of it
the perfect ass for my man & none of it is theirs
this is mine/ ntozake 'her own things'/ that's my name/
(Shange 1976, 49)

Shange uses the slash mark to temporarily rein in her line, catch her breath, and get ready for the next ultimatum. She wants on-goingness, nonstop assault, and praise: she wants energetic truth-telling, pushing forward with no codified punctuation to make it look nicer than it is. She doesn't want to leave any room for back talk or interruption, which is out there waiting to erase her, lock her out, hush her up, or sweet-talk her into giving in and giving over her "stuff." With these slashes for pause, a less restrained momentum pushes the line forward, embodying her slang and the liveliness of her speech rhythms. One's attention is turned relentlessly to the field of material being presented. Everything in that field is pitched at a fairly equal intensity, flooding from a mind and body moving fluidly among the multiple grievances it intends to unload and making room for the carefully noted details that crowd in along the way. This formal solution to an onrushing, urgent desire to get across her demands in the face of harassment, provides a model of writing that couldn't have been mapped in quite this way by anyone unexperienced in the daily demands being made upon a young black woman. It frees Shange from both a thralldom to her lover/oppressor and to the more subtle claims of the polite rules of prosody.

.

Breaking and entering a field of energy, taking on meaning at any particular point, is an important concept informing Maureen Owen's linear structure for her book-length work, *Amelia Earhart*. Owen has written in her "Working Notes" for this project:

Flat geographies can be invented w/intersecting and meandering
waters that are little stories merging from different sources & what

happens is writing where the process of the poem being written becomes the actual poem & the actual poem becomes the process of the poem being written. All the wrong words are part of it too then & the spaces between the words breathe because there is no finished poem just all that goes into it. (Owen 1983, 2)

In this statement, the influences of Charles Olson's attention to breath as pause ("& the spaces between the words breathe because there is no finished poem") mark an individual poet transmitting her peculiar energy, voice, and pulse through the measure of her line and its "breathing." We also recognize the New York School's valuing of process—its stops and starts, its common and uncommon moments included in the action of the poem (the painting) as part of its shape and texture on the page.

But Owen takes these ideas and brings to them her desire to "fly," to free herself from the confines of literal interruption by her children's ever-present claims and their inability to imagine, in any equal way, the need for concentrated silence and continuity of thought by this person, their mother-caretaker. It is not just that an Olson or O'Hara has given Owen permission to validate her process, but that their aesthetic ideas fit with the frustrating, broken, and repetitive character of her hours given over to child-tending. So while her broken, "breathing" line may resemble theirs, it is actually mapping something central to female socializing and the female experience of time—that which is a continuous series of interruptions—rather than simply "biology."

In the glamorous and independent and non-maternal figure of Amelia Earhart—flyer—Owen finds pleasure and escape from her own mundane moments by allowing her imagination to take on the personae of both "AE" and her lover and to adventure with them, expanding the variables through factual and fictionalized intimacies of history:

"Assholes!" her eyes seem grey in this soup   the hangers
chalk   &   grey   sound of the engines grey   & far off   I
craved those fogged-in afternoons   just the two of us   getting
high   &   hanging out   We'd work on the Electra   some

have a beer or two   then share our last joint   under the fuselage
& shoot the breeze   the reward for marriage is getting a
man's name   we decided   Mrs Donald Roscoe Jr.   Mrs
Kenneth Norton the III   Vowing the next time we ran   into
Ginger & Tootie   on the street   we'd hail them   as   Don!
& Ken!   the old levitation trick   first anger crushes
then leaves you   light as air   arm   squashed into doorjam
step out   & up it goes   Finally we'd laugh til we were sick
guffawing   out of control   going spaz in the spilled beer   &
oil   hugging   pawing each other wildly   we'd laugh til
we sloshed   tumbling in spilt motor oil   spazing out we'd
laugh til we were sick   pouring the rest of the beer   in
each other's hair   hugging & sloshing in spilled motor oil—
We always.   wore khakis & boots.   & if I smoked   I'd
tuck my deck   in my rolled   t shirt sleeve   the way poets
do   or stash a homemade behind my ear   like in the films
While   AE'd stand out there   in   visibility   zero
Hooting   the long letters of her name   A M E L I A........
EARHART ....
                      aviator   aviator   aviator
                      (Owen 1984, unpaged)

Cirrus, filmy scatterings of cloud and bits of light break through this backdrop of sky Owen has created in her lines for Amelia. One feels slight breezes, shifting surfaces and planes, layers of experience, bits and pieces of floating in the mind space/sky space of Amelia's world. Owen's line lets you inside its life, its awkwardness, its unfinished plot:

then leaves you   light as air   arm   squashed into doorjam

It lets you hear *arm.* See *arm,* in that pause. Then lets you hear *doorjam.* See it. There is a savoring of shifting perspective, an unrushed delight in the odd imperfections of unofficial, unimportant moments. No grand climax, no final victory or summing-up by the end of the book. Owen's bottom line is an investigative reporting of imagined events. A woman wants to fly, takes on the male domain in which to attempt it. This woman is at the margins of culture and history, an unfinished woman, facing the centers of power, the mysteries, her own fear and her will to break its hold on her.

"One Hundred and Three Chapters of Little Times": Collapsed and transfigured moments in the cubist fiction of Barbara Guest

And there are nervous
people who cannot manufacture
enough air and must seek
for it when they don't have plants,
in pictures. There is the mysterious
traveling that one does outside
the cube and this takes place
in air.

— Barbara Guest, "Roses," in *Moscow Mansions*

In her anti-narrative novel *Seeking Air* (first published in 1978 and re-printed in 1997), Barbara Guest has chronicled a remarkable struggle between her protagonist—a fantasy-prone and well barricaded urban American, Morgan Flew—and a world that refuses his control. This world is composed almost entirely of his lover, Miriam, and a doppelganger figure called Dark. Guest's subject is that which cannot be directly or simply told. We live in her characters' imaginations of each other (in the displaced subjunctive of what they *might* be, more than in the certain and deter-

---

FRAME: Miriam Fuchs and Ellen G. Friedman were co-editing a book on women's experimental fiction and asked me if I would write about a particular novel they had in mind. The work suggested didn't appeal to me—nor did it seem particularly innovative—so I asked if I could do a piece on Barbara Guest's novel *Seeking Air*—a "novel," but to my mind a work of high innovation employing many poetic devices. They were skeptical, not having heard of it, but let me try. Since the book had never been reviewed—the small-press problem—their ignorance of the book was not unusual. Princeton University Press, their publisher, was concerned because my essay had no footnotes. "Where would one turn for footnotes?" I asked. The essay appeared in Miriam Fuchs and Ellen G. Friedman, eds., *Breaking the Sequence: Women's Experimental Fiction* (Princeton, N.J.: Princeton University Press, 1989).

mined world of traditional narrative where one is given fully reasoned explanations and familiar conversations).

To enter into Morgan Flew's mind is to collapse or fly apart with him, to hide inside the intricacies of his hedged bets, to understand from the beginning that we are not to be granted the fictional coherence of knowing "everything" of his origins and reasons for being. Instead, Guest has brought to her novelistic experiment the practiced hand of the collagist, the eye of a film editor and a word-on-word attention to *constructed* reality that marks the modernist poetic sensibility.

Drawing on her years of association with the New York School—as poet, collagist, and art critic—Guest has appropriated visual solutions proposed by European and American artists who prefigured (and influenced) abstract expressionism. Her intention is to create a disrupted narrative text, and through this, to underscore the fragility and ambivalence of her characters' personae in the world. Within this context she has forged a strikingly innovative fictional model based on discrete units and intervals, strengthened by peculiar juxtapositions that resemble certain cubist paintings or experimental films in their overlapping planes and abrupt shifts.

Guest consciously situates her book in the spirited tradition of Virginia Woolf's later novels and, to some degree, Dorothy Richardson's prose (wherein the abstinence from conventional plot and the avoidance of verifiable climax mark an escape route from determined consequence). But instead of Woolf's expanding perceptions or Richardson's circuitous full-blown revelations, Guest opts for the half-seen clue, the private notation, the broken surface, and the fleeting thought as they collide, impinge upon, and elucidate one another.

Her genius lies in the poetic compression she brings to the text. Whereas her structuralist/cubist perspective provides the innovative frame for *Seeking Air,* her prose diction proposes a contrast of almost nineteenth century formality and limpidity. Her sentences are classic; her experiment is, rather, how she puts them together. Like the cubists, she has not given up the elegant brushwork, the good painting. Her book aims an affectionate salute at the history of English prose, while at the same time making a conscious critique—or departure from—its literary formalisms, extending our idea of how narrative "truth" can be delivered.

An introduction to Guest's working method throughout the novel can be made by considering the character and scale of her "chapters," usually from one paragraph to five pages in length. Each chapter in *Seeking Air* provides a new cut in the crystal, a clue or a book of clues. There are passages whose energies are sustained by the sheer speed of metaphor, the humor derived from surprised couplings:

> Berg changes to Shostakovitch. The Cyrillic alphabet just out, crosses in front of, enters the space the bus vacated. The poem laughs back and forth and comes the caw-like repetition. Strength comes to blows with Joy. The violins fly from steppe to steppe and in the Caucasus valleys stones skim and fall. A stocky tremolo with light flashing on the flung scabbards. Numbers work for you. Desire trudging beyond the golden mean. (Guest 1978, 119)

The shortest chapter is composed of a fragment, a half-sentence with ellipses—"This diary of a place . . ." (W. S. Graham)—and is meant as a notation on her aesthetic intentionality. It echoes the epigraph of *Seeking Air,* in which Jonathan Swift amuses himself by proposing, in a letter to his friend, Vanessa, a plan for a new sort of novel:

> It ought to be an exact chronicle of twelve years from the time of spilling the coffee to drinking of coffee. From Dunstable to Dublin with every single passage since . . . two hundred chapters of madness, the chapter of long walks, the Berkshire surprise, fifty chapters of little times.

One feels an enormous empathy and attraction between Swift's sensibility—the scale and location of his passions—and Guest's as she hunts down not only the spilled coffee, the chapters of madness, and the "little times" but also the elusive language in which to snare them. Her "long walks" are discovered on city terraces, not in the Irish countryside; her "madness" chapters locate themselves in the narcissism of Morgan's inbred fantasies—for example, his imagined seduction by a woman in a blue dress, painted by Ingres, staring down at him from a wall in the Frick

Museum. Her "Berkshire surprise" is an unexpected indoor picnic of tinned white asparagus and other gourmet items squirreled away by city-dwelling Morgan.

Guest quotes Swift in order to set the stage for her own compositional scale, in which certain moments will be foregrounded and heightened, others abstracted or reduced, refusing the more conventional novelistic balance and proportion. She wants to remind us that the investigation of human nature has resulted in a variety of narrative solutions. From this perspective — this sense of scale — she will build the lives of her characters, leaving ample room for mystery and abstraction.

Guest's fictional surfaces are further complicated by her whimsical homage to other literary genres, a device that reinforces the reader's awareness of multiple and skewed time frames. Tiny metafictions appear inside the ongoing story of Morgan and Miriam: after a difficult course of love and a prolonged separation, they are suddenly featured in a little Shakespearean comedy scene called "Act the First," in which they say their healing lines, but in voices thrice removed from the late twentieth-century language one might expect following a lover's quarrel:

> M[iriam]: *'Tis odd. Though I long for homeland yet loathe am I to leave this land. An enchantment lieth here that graspeth still my girdle.*

> M[organ]: *A like feeling steals o'er me. 'Tis as if we live half awake and half in dream. The dream is here and there awakeness tarries. Yet must I shake this dream and hasten to the harbour.*

> M[iriam]: *Sweet was our rest, though troubled by Eustace's sorrow. That lent a shadow to our ends.* (174)

Critical distance is created between reader and romantic plot through dislocation of the present moment, and one's perception of surface unity dissolves.

In another "genre" scene, Morgan and Miriam reestablish their intimacy through the staged ritual of cooking a meal together, discovering

and replaying their own private style of amusement while consulting instructions from a 1930s cookbook in which each recipe, each gesture in
the kitchen, is thoroughly laced with appropriate attitudes, clichéd lines,
and reassurances once widespread in the institutions of American domes-
ticity. The reader is not told how or why this happens but is, instead, given
chunks of the literal cookbook text verbatim:

> *Creamed tuna on toast strips*
> *Canned peas with butter sauce*
> *rolls   butter*
> *Strawberry preserves*
> *Hot chocolate with marshmallows*
> (144)

The recasting of Morgan's and Miriam's reconciliation deflects what
could be a predictable exchange and colors it with historic precedent,
treating the reader to apposed perceptions, socialized and historically changing love-scripts. Guest's layering of what we think of as time-bound experience tilts our expectations, much as the shifting cubist planes of a Juan
Gris interior can alert the eye to multiple perspectives of the material
world, challenging traditional assumptions. Guest's affinity for the clue, the
allusive fragment, contributes to the modeling and revelation of her characters. She names her female character Miriam, after Dorothy Richardson's
Miriam in *Pilgrimage*. In a kind of homage to Richardson, which is also a
revision, Guest rigorously edits what might be a very long and program-
matically detailed narrative script into a more poetic structure of swift cuts
and enigmatic dialogues, which are never meant to be fully explained.
Duplicating the blow-by-blow nature of "real" time is not her goal. However, the homage may not be immediately apparent partly because the
luxuriant winds and turns of Richardson's sentences in *Pilgrimage* are located in the female monologue.

The voice of Richardson's Miriam is urgent in its attempt to understand and break with the confining social expectations that flood and di-
minish her. In Guest, this question is displaced by the fact that Morgan, the

male protagonist, is the seer. Guest's Miriam, while sharing a similar passion to resist category and interpretation, is seen from a cooler, spliced
perspective because the point-of-view is predominantly Morgan's, and
Morgan is never of a single mind, but awash with disintegrating memories
and shifting discriminations. He is an obsessive man, out of step with his
time, and locked into a self-absorption so delicious that it threatens to
reduce his days to collapsed past events at the expense of his tenuous hold
on the present "real" world—particularly as regards Miriam, whom he
tends to see at a slight and somewhat literary remove. He must assure
himself that he has the upper hand in their relationship; his perspective
cannot admit to her strength nor her separate life outside his imagination.
We are made to feel the paradox of his situation since we come to know
Miriam as a "successful" contemporary woman, yet find this fact slipping
away from us given Guest's narrative design. Miriam is not often allowed a
direct comment in *Seeking Air*. Her attachment to Morgan sustains the
unresolved mystery of the book. But this is part of Guest's strategy. She has
turned Richardson's telescope around, we are not given the certain advan-
tage of Miriam's longing for presence and authenticity through continuous access to *her* interiority. Instead, we are looking at a contemporary
Miriam through the multiple projections of her male lover. Rather than
locating us chiefly inside *her* sensibility, we are primarily privileged to a
view of her from the book's narrator who appears to claim objectivity,
even as he exposes the fragility of his psyche. Morgan's questionable authority is presented and then dismantled. The sacred tablet of objective
narrative is shattered.

Although they handle it differently, Guest and Richardson share a love
of the elaborate interior monologue. Guest shifts perspectives as one might
shift camera angles to render missing information. In the middle of Morgan's
self-serving observation, we are quite suddenly allowed to enter Miriam's
mind. One feels she is outwitting the ever-watchful Morgan in this brief
reflection that must be hers, though its tone would appear to be impersonal:

> If idly she were to go out onto the terrace and from the snow
> take a snowball. A snowball and hurtle it through the air. Could it

truly be said that for a few seconds that snowball had been hers, the choice had been made freely by her, Miriam, to throw it into the air? Or would Morgan when she told him what she had done, would he create another action out of hers, would he call it a performance, would he make of the terrace a stage, would he deprive her even of the scenery by causing a scene to take place between the woman alone on the terrace and the snow held in her hand? (84)

Morgan's need to appropriate Miriam's experience — to edit it along the lines of his Pygmalion script for her — is at odds with other views we have of her. A quick gloss of Miriam shows her as self-directed and self-sufficient. Yet she is still lonely for Morgan when away from him. Again, we are refused the ease of narrative in favor of multiple readings.

The other effect of this is to cast Miriam in the dilemma that is classic to modern woman. She craves autonomy, self-determination, yet feels partial without the constancy of a primary love. Miriam's fragmented and unstable perception of herself is aligned with ours, because her character structure is parallel to and supported by the overall narrative plan of the book. Miriam is seeking the air of her own spontaneous choices, the adventure of discovering who she might become, independent of a primary relationship. But she is also compelled and moved by Morgan's passion, his imagination, his apparent confidence as he navigates the world. At the same time, she often feels engulfed by his admiration and devoted smothering of her tentative self-rule. Morgan seeks reprieve, escape from a rule-bound and competitive regime only hinted at. Miriam's substantiality, her grace in negotiating daily life, holds for Morgan the promise of pleasurable relief and allows him to avoid his own struggle with the dark forces threatening him.

Clearly, our understanding of Miriam's dilemma — her tenuous hold on her own identity and autonomy — is being shaped by the voice of experience. Guest enters Morgan's power base, lays bare his willfulness and his dogged recasting of the motives and intentions of his love object (Miriam) to suit his own ego-serving impulses. In this way Guest explores the baffled and ambivalent position Miriam finds herself in, vis-à-vis Morgan and their restless embarkation upon a shared life and its insidious underminings.

It is here that Guest's collapsed chapters, displaced viewpoints, reframed genres, and collaged quotations both erode and question a more traditional narrative ordering; furthermore, they enunciate her perception of time as elastic, subjective, circular, and multidimensional. Morgan is implicated, drawn into her less deterministic time frame; Guest's ease with and insistence on this perspective succeed in making of Morgan a man who struggles toward the appropriation of a woman's soul. His attempt to take over and mold Miriam's life is really an attempt to save himself.

In his Journal, Morgan concedes to his intrusive desires (his self-awareness would be admirable, if only he could align it with a different attitude toward Miriam). His desire is congruent with his need to subjugate and objectify her. He confides: "It has been noted of Karenin that: 'not until the storm is about to break does he actually concede that Anna might have her own destiny, thoughts, desire . . .'"; and then he continues:

> My attitude toward Miriam was interwoven with my preoccupation with her as a person whom first I had discovered and then one who I believed I might recreate in the image I desired. It can be said to my distress that I never let her alone. I persistently meddled with her character. I left her only to solitude. When with her, that is in the same room with her, my imagination infused itself into desire. Osip Mandelstam's wife explains this state quite clearly when she tells us that Mandelstam's endearment for her was "my you." (72)

Morgan's very literary and dissembling mind is here revealed in three swift moves. His journal entries, their collaged sources and shifts, display his character without need of belabored analysis: in the first paragraph, he somewhat painlessly allows himself to view his refusal to accept Miriam's separate destiny, by noting another man's blindness under similar circumstances. This man appears in a Tolstoy novel, thus Morgan's lack borrows some sympathy and weight (in his mind), while linking him to a male dilemma that is obviously historical. In the second, he confesses his guilt

(within the privacy of his secret pages), admitting—but in the past tense—
that he has allowed his own egoistic needs constantly to tamper with and
attempt the reshaping of Miriam's separateness. Morgan's instinct to remove himself, even as he reveals himself, is most clearly evident in the
third section where he remembers a little story told by "Osip Mandelstam's
wife" in which her husband's term of endearment for her was "my you."
In one sentence, Morgan reduces Mandelstam's wife to both possession
and object in failing to call her by her own name. Yet *she* is the conduit for
Morgan's point. The reader, by now, has been several times removed from
Morgan's original observation, in the same fashion that he distances himself from troubling insight. He desires to know and not to know.

Perhaps Guest's most extreme use of dislocation is in the construction
of Morgan's character. She takes us beyond the monologue and into his
mental graffiti. Throughout *Seeking Air,* Guest constructs her portrait of
Morgan from the inside. She reveals pages intact from his journal, looks
into his pocket and finds a little double-columned list, and presents it as a
"chapter," prefaced by this note: "I found these . . . in my pocket, in the
jacket I had worn on that last trip to Washington. Placed there when I
picked up my nephew, Neil. The second column was my own addenda":

In case of illness or absence for any other	expectancy, forgiveness, betrayal,
cause, please notify the school as soon as	detective stories, paintings, lights
possible. In an emergency in the morning,	(electric), buying paper, pens, post-
please call your driver between 7: 15 and....	office, heels of shoes fixed, the
7:30	river, the sun....(76)

The reader is asked to make sense of, to participate in Morgan's private
order, bits of detritus from the street and from his mind's foraging. We
begin to build up an actively shifting picture of our protagonist, a less static
view of him than if we were directed smoothly through the difficult chan-
nels of his life by a single observing voice. Guest's collaged perspective
gives us a visual way of participating in Morgan's multiple and often war-
ring sides. In this instance, she places the left-hand column—"Transportation Regulations for the Sheridan School, Grades I, II, III" (evidence of his
chosen obligation to some distant family life and institutional order)—

next to a random list of words and thought fragments from his day, perhaps scrawled in a single minute or during an extended bus ride. One is invited to imagine how these bits of paper have arrived in his pocket, by the fact of their presence as material evidence. Neither the episode of picking up his nephew, Neil, nor the contents of the list requires further elaboration.

It is within Morgan's continuously observing, reasoning, chattering and obsessive mind that we are introduced to the third and in some ways major "character" of this unusual book—the presence called Dark. Morgan's story unfolds, often, through the moods and levels of his psychic journey. He talks to himself; he confides to us; he both lures and banishes his doppelganger, this insatiable haunt, Dark. While Morgan and Miriam are seeking each other and their inventions of each other, the character of Dark is always hovering in the shadows of Morgan's mind, a kind of vampire of the present moment who divides and often conquers Morgan's attention. Dark is "not the thing, but its effect" (Mallarmé), a ghostly projection, carbon paper's smudge, Morgan's comforting pillow, *and* his resistance to a world he finds too demanding and often not as interesting as his own daydreaming. He prefers his fantasies, his lineage among the gazelles, his continuously revised histories (he likes to think of himself as the war hero, the gentleman planter).

Dark encourages Morgan in this activity and is his caustic but reliable phantom companion. Morgan works at Dark like a text, almost a biography. He gathers research notes, goes into retreat, pursues his subject shamelessly. We are never really sure whether Dark is a literal manuscript he is working on or a perpetual (ongoing) narrative in his head. Where his "writing" takes place is always in question. Miriam and close friends shift between tolerantly assuming a place for Dark at every table or being frustrated and appalled by Morgan's obsessive pursuit.

Morgan claims that his colleagues take the easier path of "grey" or "beige" and believes his investment is in something much deeper:

> And I returned to "Dark's" exegesis. Which if ever finished I
> shall deliver No. 3 in the series of "Evenings Of and About Litera-
> ture." Transforming the wild evenings of Alaska into something
> less raw, translating the kayak noise into black clefs, white floes

into Dark. Don't tremble Miriam when I put the bandage over your eyes; we shall only slide into the underground. And we can read standing up the gold emblems of Dark. A nest of swallows clinging to the sooty bridge. (25)

Morgan's thralldom to Dark assumes mythic proportions and is, at the same time, annoying. Guest's accomplishment is that, amid her filmic fades and close-ups, she provokes our concern for her protagonist's embattled psyche while, at the same time, accusing him of infantile Wertherian excesses completely unsuitable to the man we want for Miriam. Morgan anguishes: "Why must I be so constant to Dark, tracing its outline everywhere like a prisoner his shadow?" and we wince at his romantic self-indulgence. Soon after, Guest interposes a little answering chapter, a kind of tonic to Morgan's angst, a scene in which Miriam discovers Morgan's unawareness of a piece of disturbing news in the morning paper: "Yet you did hear about it—didn't you?" A dialogue follows, in which his numbness to an exterior world of people and events becomes evident. Miriam finally comments in exasperation: "You must be living in a private world entirely" and he counters: "Doesn't everyone?" (122).

She refuses his simple equation: "Oh of course if you put it that way, but most people try at one point or other to get outside themselves, they even want to become involved with others" (122). Nothing is settled, but the question is on the table. A brief moment of exchange serves beyond simple character development: to implicate the reader in the dialogue and to discourage dependency on authorial finality and closure. One can draw a conclusion, shift allegiances, feel the priority of either attitude.

Guest imagines her reader as curious and avid for the pleasure of active intellection; she asks us to approach her juxtaposed lists, events, quotes, and bits of interior monologue in the same way we stand before a cubist painting of a [tablewindowpipeguitar] by Braque or a Joseph Cornell three-dimensional box, in which a blue-and-white map of the Northern Celestial Hemisphere is placed as a background for six wine glasses, an opaque glass "shooter" marble, and two bluish-white Italian marble spheres—to suggest (among other things) the earth twice seen from a great distance.

In *Seeking Air,* we must put together a "meaning" via the subject's angles, materials, functions, and planes; we must read the gaps, the overlapping clues.

Miriam's life force and the spirit of poetry finally triumph, albeit tentatively, in this complicated dance. Miriam provides Morgan with materiality, an engaged world of both playfulness and fury in which to receive the present moment. Conversely, Morgan gives Miriam access to the inaccessible, the claims of mythic time. She becomes his white page, he her dark script. Guest has personified two orientations toward life, finally hinting at a difficult shift for Morgan from perpetual brooding to a somewhat lighter and dynamic possibility. Dark is jilted and "White" begins to appear as a presence and a tonality of experience. White is absence of shadow. White is Miriam dozing on the couch, her perfume.

Morgan struggles to *get* it. He characteristically stays up all night in an insomniac battle to incorporate this new element, so long eluding his grasp. He mumbles, and it is poetry:

> Dark being edged out by White.
> Impossible!
> I had thought if I could insert a fleecy thing Dark might find more comfort. Instead I kept finding white threads, and worse white soft lumps like cotton. Comfortable, undoubtedly, but *white.* And the white multiplied so fast. Dark the tyrant, Dark the fastidious, kept turning his back, refusing to face that at all. (180)

And he continues:

> Yet wait. White had appeared very late in the game. There had been intimations. The quarrels. The disputes. The bad timing. It had not been until he had sensed, vaguely sensed a need for, or a lack of, the Whiteness. . . . Until he had recognized the wholeness of White. It had taken some catching up and a degree of modesty unusual for him. Also a humility to accept Dark's real even urgent need for White. (183)

Mere mortals these, Morgan and Miriam, in whose modern yet timeless souls Guest has waged the battle of the century: loving versus selfhood, partnership without ownership. What has resisted closure is finally disclosed. Those bound to the earth will always seek "the mysterious / traveling that one does outside / the cube and this takes place / in air" (Guest 1973, "Roses," 59).

Translating the unspeakable:
Visual poetics, as projected through Olson's
"field" into current female writing practice

> ... all from tope/type/trope, that built in is the connec-
> tion, in each of us, to Cosmos. ...
>
> Place (topos, plus one's own bent plus what one *can* know,
> makes it possible to
> name.
>
> —Charles Olson, "Letter to Elaine Feinstein," May 1959

"When I was a child, my grandmother used to mix a paste for me of flour and water. Then I would go out into the yard and pick grass and make drawings out of pencil and grass pasted to the paper" (Norma Cole). "When I was writing, I was imagining that one side of the paper was folded over onto the other and that some words got stuck ... as if they were wet ... or more alive and would come loose and stick to the other page" (Susan Gevirtz). "Language was a fluid surface full of juxtapositions and collisions and swirls ... like an ocean, in the sense that it didn't lend itself to a linear, determined kind of construction. So the idea of spatial composition gave me a way of approaching writing" (Mary Margaret Sloan).

FRAME: In the late summer of 1996, "Assembling Alternatives"—a major international conference of English-language poets and scholars particularly compelled by innovative practice—was convened at the University of New Hampshire under the direction of Romana
Huk. Many of the poet participants were asked to present papers, as well as to give poetry
readings, as a way of sharing descriptions of working method and newly imagined poetic
practice. I decided to trace the path of visual influence inherited by women innovators
who connected powerfully to Charles Olson's freeing of the page as a graphic site for
poetic composition. A condensed version of this piece was later published in *Moving
Borders: Three Decades of Innovative Writing by Women*, edited by Mary Margaret Sloan
(Jersey City, N.J.: Talisman House, 1998).

These recent depictions of early intuitive beginnings describe a longing to make visible one's own peculiar way of experiencing how the mind moves and how the senses take note. Longing craves articulation and, in cases such as these, has sought out visual apparatus as scaffolding on which to construct formerly inarticulate states of being. Expanding onto the FULL PAGE—responding to its spatial invitation to play with typographic relations of words and alphabets, as well as with their denotative meanings, has delivered visual-minded poets from the closed, airless containers of the well-behaved poem into a writing practice that foregrounds the investigation and pursuit of the unnamed. The dimensionality of the full page invites multiplicity, synchronicity, elasticity . . . perhaps the very female subjectivity proposed by Julia Kristeva as linking both cyclical and monumental time.

If monumental longing were joined to cyclical writing practice, how would a poet nursed on Left-margin poetics go about describing this both/ and condition? Would it be like describing light, in both its wave *and* particle manifestation? I think so. What has been left out of the poetic account of women in time is now manifestly present through the developing use of the page as a four-sided document. Such poetry focuses on the visual potential of the page for collage, extension, pictorial gesture and fragmentation—language and the silence that surrounds it, constellations of word and phrase that embody and signal the poem's range of intention . . . extending far beyond a mere clever manipulation of signs.

However, the *visualized* topos of interior speech and thought—that full or fully empty arena of the page imagined into being by a significant number of non-traditional women poets now publishing—cannot really be adequately thought about without acknowledging the immense, permission-giving moment of Charles Olson's "PROJECTIVE VERSE" manifesto (widely circulated from 1960 onward, through its paperback arrival in Donald Allen's *The New American Poetry*). There is no doubt that— even if arrived at through a subtle mix of osmosis and affinity* rather than a direct reading of Olson's manifesto—poets entering literature after 1960

---

* Cynthia Hogue defines affinity as "a shared spiritual and erotic set of valuings" (Hogue 1998).

gained access to a more expansive page through Olson's own visual enactment of "field poetics," as mapped out in his major exploratory work, *The
Maximus Poems.*

An urgency toward naming, bringing voice to off-the-record thought
and experience — as marked by increasing eccentricities of syntax, cadence,
diction, and tone — would have lacked such a clear concept of PAGE as
canvas or screen on which to project flux without the major invitation
Olson provided . . . this, in spite of his territorial inclusive/exclusive boy-
talk. The excitement Olson generated, the event of the *making* — the hands-
on construction of a poem being searched out, breathed into and lifted
through the page, fragment by fragment, from the archeological layers of
each individual's peculiar life — revealed the complex grid of the maker's
physical and mental activity. Its *it.*

Susan Howe has noted that "Olson's *acute visual sensitivity* separates *The
Maximus Poems* from *The Cantos* and *Paterson* . . ." (Howe 1987, 5) — two
other models for poets writing in the 1960s who desired to break from a
more standardized poem model. Olson's idea of high energy "projection"
engaged an alchemy of colliding sounds and visual constructions, valuing
*ir*regularity, counterpoint, adjacency, ambiguity . . . the movement of poetic language as investigative tool. An open field, not a closed case.

Olson's declared move away from the narcissistically probing, psychological defining of self — so seductively explored by Sylvia Plath, Anne
Sexton, and Robert Lowell in the early and mid-Sixties, and by their avid
followers for at least a generation after — helped to provide a major alter-
native ethic of writing for women poets who resisted the "confessional"
model for their poems. While seriously committed to gender consciousness, a number of us carried an increasing skepticism toward any *fixed*
rhetoric of the poem, implied or intoned. We resisted the prescription of
authorship as an exclusively unitary proposition — the essential "I" positioned as central to the depiction of reflectivity.

As antidote to a mainstream poetics that enthusiastically embraced those
first I-centered poems, Olson (in "Projective Verse") had already proposed:

> the getting rid of the lyrical interference of the individual as ego,
> of the "subject" and his soul, that peculiar presumption by which

western man has interposed himself between what he is as a creature of nature (with certain instructions to carry out) and those
other creations of nature. . . . (in Allen 1960, 395)

The excitement and insistence of Olson's spatial, historical, and ethical
margins, while clearly speaking from male imperatives, nevertheless helped
to stake out an arena whose initial usefulness to the poem began to be
inventively explored by American women—in some cases drastically re-
conceived, beginning with work in the 1960s and 1970s by such poets as
Susan Howe and Hannah Weiner and continuing forward to very recent
poetry by women just beginning to publish.

It is useful to compare several of Olson's graphic "signatures" with a
sampling of pages wherein women poets have claimed that spatial and
typographic mandate for entirely different uses and meanings—notations
mapped directly out of the very lives Olson tended to discredit by his act
of non-address. The occasion of the empty page became, for them, an
open canvas; a "screen of distance" (Guest 1989, 35); a grave of memory;
the template above a door of hidden resolve; another kind of use value; a
"forehead" on which to scrawl a new language; the recovery of lost grammars of women written over; a slate on which to collage and draw and
reconfigure the lessons of "the master teacher."

The page contained even a topos of silence and emptiness, a briefest
hint or suggested nuance; a record of temporality—its continuously broken surfaces, its day-by-day graphs of interruption and careening (the speed
and intermingling of the brain's bits and layers), perhaps less deeply tat-
tooed with marks of ownership than historically endorsed formal models.
These new pages have often been claimed as the location where an entirely "inappropriate" or "inessential" content might be approached or seized,
by fact of the poet's very redefining of margin as edge: four margins, four
edges—PAGE in place of the dictated rigor and predictable pull of the
straight, the dominant Flush Left.

I don't believe that a single woman poet who entered this "field" knew,
ahead of time, precisely how or what she would project into/onto its emptiness, nor how that field would assist in producing these works—writings
projected from immense necessity *to make* as well as to express—with

their infinite grids, mathematical strategies, random patterns and ciphers. In this sense, it was Olson's urgency to expand graphically into that open space (further enabled by Robert Duncan's lyric extension of "the field") that so importantly provided many contemporary women with a major invitation and set of gestures to help expand poetry's topography, syllable by syllable.

But there was a second visual source at work here. In parallel time with Olson, a handful of women painters variously associated with New York abstract and expressionist movements were helping to shape and advance the 1950s/1960s graphic imagination. I refer to the innovative paintings produced by Helen Frankenthaler, Nell Blaine, Elaine DeKooning, Grace Hartigan, Agnes Martin, Jane Freilicher, and Joan Mitchell. In this context, one cannot help but rethink those first delicate grids of Agnes Martin's, pencilled over space. One is further reminded of Joan Mitchell's series called "Champs" (or "Fields"), which seem to be composed of pure energy, the brush strokes laden with luscious color, applied again and again, often with many layers of underpainting; or her "Between" series (worked on, between the larger canvases of the "Champs" sequence), small pictures in which each initially empty canvas isolated and captured a detail up-close—as in a lens marking arbitrary boundaries within which a small part of a larger, perhaps more complex and amorphous landscape can be looked at in blown-up detail.

These ideas continue to nourish and to illuminate the making of those language constructs we link to "Champs" or to field composition. It is this parallel affinity—this set of screens, grids and underpaintings—that located itself in the poetry (and, later, in the novel *Seeking Air*) of Barbara Guest, the most painterly writer of the vanguard first generation of poets gathered under the umbrella of The New York School.

With a quick look at several pages from *The Maximus Poems,* one can begin to grasp Olson's graphic intervention in the field of the regularized page. Reviewing, then, a selection of pages from the dozens of spatially innovative texts published by women during the years since the arrival of *Maximus,* one may read their alterations and detours. Whereas Olson's writing *topos* located itself, first, in and with BODY—its breath, energy, and synaptic activity—he chose to transfer his perception of all these simultaneous functions—their interdependent processes—to the page, as a kind of ledger accounting of how all parts of history and human nature move and talk with each other.

so early

Mr. Edward Johnson: "yet that there have been vessels built here at the town of late" I haven't noticed any single adult, the children however and up through 17 at least on the Fort or Fort high school men whatever hour of the day I see them even early on the Boulevard and a couple of them in uniform with rifle R.O.T.C. don't look like cowboys and English:

Stefansson's ice, what trade replaced Pytheas's sludge with, man goeth novo siberskie slovo only a Chinese feeling not Canton silk or Surinam Rose-Troup to you, Gloucester, solely gave you place in the genetic world, she said Richard Bushrod George Way etc. she put you back on the launching platform said woman said John White planter Conant said Budleigh she said Cape Ann she said dorchester company she said so much train oil   quarters of oak   skins as well as dryfish corfish   fox racons martyns otter muskuatche beaver   some even entered as 'coats' thus indicating there were Algonquins left after smallpox? It looks as though Miss Rose-Troup connects back to Champlain the number of wigwams show Freshwater Cove above Cressys in Tolmans field near Half Moon or possibly the old Steep Bank where Kent Circle   maybe it's Apple Row or Agamenticus Height

the river and marshes show clearly and no Indians along the Beach   forest on Fort Point   wigwams again at Harbor Cove in fact all up between what 1642 became the harbor and the town in other words "Washington" St to Mill River and on Fore Street to Vinsons Cove otherwise Indians about East Gloucester Square and then it's action: Champlain discovering the Indian attack to Sieur de Pountrin-court in ambush at the head of Rocky Neck, old European business as seven or eight arquebusiers   the depths of the channel more interesting as from Eastern Pt and the compass rose thus:

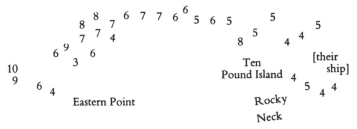

Fig. 6. From Olson 1983, 156.
The horizontal text, top, appears to be a linear narrative yet is more like a rushing forth into open space where all thought and speech and remembered detail might find room enough to be present at the same time . . . a faithful reportage of the physical history of place . . . opening above that coastline profile of numbers and names of ports; the numerical drawing of a fish; a constellation, seen in the night skies, from a fishing boat.

A <u>Maximus</u>
As of why thinking of why such questions as security, and the great white
death, what did obtain at said some such point as Bowditch the Practical
Navigator who did use Other People's Monies as different from his Own,
isn't the Actuarial the ReaL Base of Life Since, and is different From
Usury Altogether, is the Thing which made all the Vulgar Socialization
(Socialism CulturiSM LiberalISM jass is gysm) why I Don't Haven't Gotten
it all Further?

                          Pound, a person of the poem

                          Ferrini

                          Hammond

                 Stevens

                 (Griffiths)

        John Smith   fish

        Conants   ships

        Higginsons

        Bowditch   Lew Douglas   fishermen
                                 Carl Olsen
           Hawkinses   Walter Burke

                   John Burke   houses

                                                 finance
        John White
        John Winthrop   wood (ekonomikos
                                          sculpture

                             marine
                             architecture

            the plum
            the flower   The Renaissance a
                                             box

                                             the economics & poetics
                                             thereafter
                    the   God" – Agyasta?
        Cosmos   "Savage   primitive ("buttocks   the prior
                                                    etc

Fig. 7. From Olson 1983, 193.
A paragraph of mind as place . . . mapping an airy physical terrain, a screen on which to
project and gather in one place a jumble of speculation, jumping-out from historical
accounts of Olson's Gloucester home and intellectual digging ground . . . ample enough
to contain a densely patched-together mosaic of references from his reading and local
slang . . . telegraphing names across the white paper for their personal and historical
significance, but with no referents, no "helps" to the reader.

        Physically, I am home.   Polish it

The Earth—and sea level.   Now,
Heaven: be the Moon reflecting,
from the Earth the Light
(of the Sun.   Be Charles the
Product
(of the Process) as Gloucester is the Necco

            <u>necessary woman</u>   not go away

        renders service
        of an essential
     and intimate
       kind

    of the
Pragmatism (secular
cosmology, not   materials
theology of most (or highest—hypsissimus

      Tower
    of Ziggurat Mount hypsistos
Purgatory "Heaven"
   in that 7, or <u>Colored</u>
  such

    but
  saecula
saeculorum
        conditioned—<u>limited</u>
      Necessity is essential to an end (boundary   Time 82,000,000,000
        or condition (conditio   years
               founded—<u>Creation</u>
   indispensable

of this age   saeculum   a race, age, the world——and I,
Charles @ the
Vision (<u>Video</u> to   "look" View Point
see (C @ ◎ ◎   <u>skope</u>

       "<u>Height</u>"

Fig. 8. From Olson 1983, 456.
Home: the Cosmos . . . Olson's e.mail: Charles@theVision. Sixties technology. "Be Charles
the / Product / (of the Process) as Gloucester is the Necco" (the round, sweet center, the
nexus).

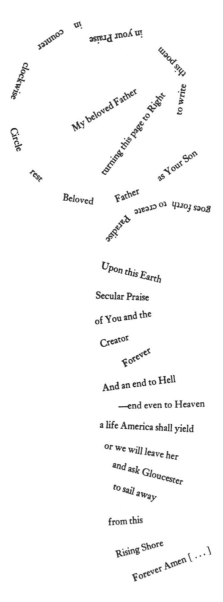

Fig. 9. From Olson 1983, 499.
Counting, clockwise . . . going backwards to celebrate the Source: "My beloved Father"
. . . prayer-wheel taking apart the house of religion . . . making his own Paradise . . .
without Milton.

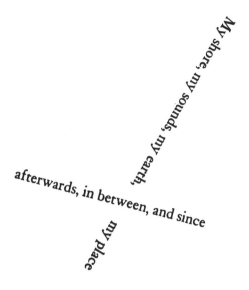

Fig. 10. From Olson 1983, 438.
Time crossing Place . . . two rhythms, one disrupted . . . laser constellation.

His cosmos was fleshed-out with double-column texts, lists, numbers, historic bits of data, proper names, uppercase WORDS, arrows > > > >, slashes ///, asterisks ★★★★★★, underscores and other enlarged graphic symbols, as well as lines of type (the typewriter being his linotype & personal computer), tilted at odd angles or flying across the page, constituting a tremendous mimetic attempt to account for the *dynamic* physical world as primary text.

•

The Olson pages (figs. 6–11), are chosen consecutively from *The Maximus Poems,* spanning work published in magazines from the late Fifties through the mid-Sixties (eventually collected into various published editions). The page numbers refer to those in the University of California Press edition (1983). One may best appreciate the work by first taking in the visual quality, the entire "field" of the PAGE.

there is

the smallest

the unit

Wed night (after 2 AM Thursday
July 16th –
'LXIX

Charles Olson

Fig. 11. From Olson 1983, 623.
cutting   and   pasting   breath.

.

The formal word-grid (fig. 12) introduced by Robert Duncan in his
poem "The Fire," published in his 1968 collection *Bending the Bow*, suspended a bridge and laid down a model that connects Olson's tumultuous
page consciousness and Agnes Martin's calmly graphed canvas to contemporary variants—word-on-word pieces (sometimes in a series)—developed since then.

THE FIRE   PASSAGES 13

jump	stone	hand	leaf	shadow	sun
day	plash	coin	light	downstream	fish
first	loosen	under	boat	harbor	circle
old	earth	bronze	dark	wall	waver
new	smell	purl	close	wet	green
now	rise	foot	warm	hold	cool

blood   disk

horizon   flame

The day at the window

the rain at the window

the night and the star at the window

Do you know the old language?

I do not know the old language.

Fig. 12. Word grid, from Robert Duncan, "The Fire," in *Bending the Bow* (New York: New Directions, 1968).

Essentially a quadrant, Duncan's poem section is formed by six columns of words to be read vertically and horizontally. It was inspired—via Pound— by Fenollosa's work on the Chinese written character as a medium for poetry, enriched by the Italian Renaissance paradigm of "the magic square." In a 1982 letter written to the Italian scholar/translator, Annalisa Goldoni,

Duncan writes:

> It was the proposition of composition by field that most struck
> me in Olson's 1950 manifesto. . . . In my notebook, I had projected
> *as an exercise* an ideogram, having in mind Pound's translation of
> Fenollosa's *Chinese Written Character.* . . . I was wondering . . . why
> . . . Pound had not written in ideograms, which I saw as constella-
> tions taking the place of sentences. . . . Not only presentation but
> *evocation of a presence* [author's italics] was my own course in the
> exercise. . . . The members [words] were felt to belong to an asso-
> ciation. . . . What presented itself belongd [sic] to an epiphanic
> imprint or template, and the complex happend [sic] in my child-
> hood . . . in my solitary play with a company of playmates. When
> I read "The Fire" correctly—I am in rhythm with my heart beat
> . . . and the space between the "words" is two heart beats . . .

From this excerpt we can imply Duncan's profound connection to
Olson's *page* as a graphically energetic site in which to manifest one's *physical* alignment with the arrival of language in the mind. This empathic
visual concurrence generated a kind of lithographic "stone," inscribed over
the next thirty-year interval, discharging both the Duncan/Olson ghost
print *and* a variety of original documentation, claiming the magnetic formal shape of the Agnes Martin grid for entirely new translations of formerly "unspeakable" material unearthed by a number of women poets in
the last two decades.

·

The first variant of this Martin "ideogram" that I know of appeared in
1978 in Barbara Guest's novel, *Seeking Air* (see fig. 5, p. 152), both as a
single-page "chapter" *and* a page of poem text, whose distilled words represent the internal monologue in the mind of her main female character,
Miriam. Guest's Miriam is a postmodern soulmate to Dorothy Richardson's
Miriam in *Pilgrimage,* who tastes the world with a primary sensual pleasure,
noting and naming its separate qualities of air, light, and foliage. This radiant certainty is destabilized by a second quadrant, below it, of densely
packed sentences, juxtaposing an equally present world of menacing yet

S

| | rebuke | boyne | | |
| | | | | |

churn   alpha   bet   a   keep

1727   expose   blade   broken   hid

pierce   hang   sum

clear   hester   quay   Liberties   46

tense   whisper   here   libel   foam

print   pen   dot   i   still

hole   yew   skip   1.

Fig. 13. From Susan Howe, "The Liberties," in *Defenestration of Prague* (New York: The Kulchur Foundation, 1983).

seemingly familiar imagery delivered by dream. It is this press of both realities simultaneously held in "the mind" of the page that Guest delivers so powerfully.

Figure 13 is from Susan Howe's serial work, "The Liberties," appearing first as a pamphlet (1980) and published three years later as the second half of *The Defenestration of Prague*. In this work, an elaborate series of exchanges is carried out between Jonathan Swift's companion, Stella, and William Shakespeare's character, Cordelia, who act as Howe's "ghosts and guides" as she's writing. "I think I wanted to abstract them from 'masculine' linguistic configuration," she's written. "In the psychic sphere theories fall to the ground" (Howe 1987). This page, *S,* is Stella's and may be read as her

sky	field	box	mistakes and hesitancy
			she pays attention
bowl	abrasion	tangent	setting tesserae
			a solitary, contribution of the music
paper	throat	shade	the role of tension frilled
			shredded against
			is a passionate stance

Fig. 14. From Dale Going, *Or Less* (Mill Valley: EM Press, 1991).

voice in hiding—a literal cry of isolation—choked off, reduced to en-coded speech, beginning with "rebuke" and ending with *1*.

Figure 14 was written and hand-set by Dale Going, then printed at her own Em Press as the chapbook, *Or Less* (1991). The book's epigraph is from Helen Frankenthaler: "But it kept getting more and more *beautiful* in the wrong way." The word-field is one of nine pages—each a variation on whatever word (of the nine words making up the grid) was em-bold-ened in the field of the page. That word is then responded to in the facing text.

Laura Moriarty's "Birth of Venus" (*Symmetry* 1996) imbeds its matrix inside the body of the poem which narrates a determination to inhabit the present, while marking absence—in this case, two words that *did* exist as evidenced by two word spaces, now empty, in an otherwise regularized grid (fig. 15).

•

Now I'd like to look briefly at work in which the *absence* of reliable matter (as it represents meaning) is given visual body. One notes visual affinities with Olson, in recent poems (pages) by women while often en-countering quite different individual and social agendas. Considering the page from "Primer" (fig. 16) in Myung Mi Kim's book, *The Bounty,* the reader is asked to visualize a slate of learning where a foreign-born child, once colonized and now at the borders of a new language and culture, is attempting to understand how the letter "g" connects to words and mean-

THE BIRTH OF VENUS

As a rosary
As a crucifix
She recreates the senses
Is held

coarse	vast	cast	station
stand		livery	emblem
sewn	start	laid	
bright	case	brine	stet

Eve writes a letter
Grief she says forget me
In waves beaded with foam
It falls over her dress

Fig. 15. From Laura Moriarty, "The Birth of Venus," in *Symmetry* (Penngrove, Calif.: Avec Books, 1996).

ings in English. The contrast between rationally related words and *g-words,* "incoherently" paired, evokes in one glance the deep confusion and isolation of this cultural position. It is a translation of the unspeakable, the pain of not knowing if you are understood.

In this passage, to claim one's voice would be to feel *unsafe,* in either language . . . to feel divided, fragmented, at the mercy of two competing authorities. Kim attempts to negotiate the passage between Korean, her mother tongue — the cultural memories it carries — and her second language, English, learned at age seven when her family immigrated to the

[g]

dwell a longer somnolent

g is for girl   *g* is for glove   distinguish decipher

g is for golden   first grind

sickness alter hunger   glower scour remnant

gumbling ransom   bran poison

must custom   ear left

roam willow stick   pen hearing

Fig. 16. From Myung Mi Kim, "Primer," in *The Bounty* (Minneapolis: Chax Press, 1996).

United States. To this is added the counterpoint of her fascination with linguistics and the pronunciation of letters . . . how these are represented. She translates even her method of investigation, adopting the Korean system of pronunciation, Hangul (developed in 1443), as her primer or study book, using it—with the slate of the full page—to construct her own bilingual, ambivalence-laden meanings.

Seemingly incoherent—yet "known language," in which the *absence* of traditional grammatical representation is given visual body—entirely fills the field of the mind/page (fig. 17), in Hannah Weiner's *Clairvoyant Journal,*

4 29   la   *for the book*

Dear Malcolm   **I LIKE APOSTROPH**ES

Your name just appeared about 8 feet *long* across the wall of the room close *on the*
page to the ceiling 8 feet long *you* there they are, you *me* refuse to type without them LOOK
AROUND so you return to bed and see MAKE ME A SWEATER nuts make one
yourself the last TIME NOT READY you started a letter to you HANNAH I
LOVE YOU (hanging in the kitchen air) it said *clean your apt* YOUR MOTHER
and *wear dungarees*   *oh*h these words appear BIG RHYS OPERA that's Mike
not alright June everything ^{a}n$_n$$_a$ is a clue or an order or writing *not so take a walk*
Bernadette where's the *clues* ^{ah} The underlines and caps I see   HEAL ME
oversensitive
You I hear this but usually *ugly see Joan* stomach problem YOU'LL HIT ME sure
NEGATIVE was glad to find   *not in the winter be grateful*   that was an ESP
term your name SO WHAT has been appearing around here a lot so it's in this
book JUNIOR some publisher is looking at it now *big question stop typing* BIG
11. look, it's 11 oclock   *check   not buying anything* SEE DONDE trying to
make a copy of the original it's *see danger* NOT POSSIBLE   Heard your voice
say HERE PUS last summer? COME IN JUNE it says in cat colors   And
somewhere after book NOT CONSCIOUS with the NOT in a reddish glow   NOT
RHYS   GO TO THE DENTIST   COMPLIMENT RHYS That's usually reverse
RHYS IS A BIG PROBLEM   TALK TO ME   How are you: Write to me
what on earth CALL ME   BIG DEAL   *dearest Malcolm* TOOTS DONT STOP
is a shout from the window *you heard* labor day   Can you heal from a *distance Mars* are
you NOT WHEN image of long nosed dog appears on cat, golden brown color
similar to dachshund, *not a retriever John Giorno had* cancer *lie down in his ball*
CANCEL   ASPIRIN *not cream not a compliment dont smoke*   YOU BIG
RHYS MOTHER   *get the message*   Sun moon in VIRGO VERY STRONG
YOU SEE LES LEVINE   COLLUSION IN APRIL   Will you explain what
you meant by WRITE   SIT DOWN   BIG HONEYMOON   The phone has
lots of words on it HANG UP BIG IMPOSSIBLE tells when to call who   *when* It
says CALL___ didn't realize that was an esp term too   *feel the negative* NOT
TIME TO GO WED TO THE BOWERY is that an order or someone else's
thought? *direction* hear Jackson MacLow's voice *say* that   Been drinking
cucumber juice for calcium I'm calcium deficient DONT OMIT PALESTINE go
to the SHOTS bedroom   Bob calls through a window USE HIS CUCUMBER
blender CAN YOU BOB DONT FORGIVE RHYS   Sometimes the negatives
have a low energy feeling appear in red *go slow express dont complain* WITH
RHYS hear his voice *so what* see a picture *almost* IT'S DIFFERENT these words appear a
few YUCATAN inches off the page in front of the keys NO CAT   There's NOT
TODAY too much confusion *in my mind* YOUR STOMACH   I get sick all the
time. can't get over the flus *medical   not cleansing   Hey, write*
                                                                    sign
WHO IS MALCOLM BESANT

Fig. 17. From Hannah Weiner's *Clairvoyant Journal* (New York: Angel Hair Books, 1974).

whose jacket features a photo of Weiner's forehead painted with the message I SEE WORDS. The word density encountered by the reader is an actual projected simulation of Weiner's multiple language tracks, activated by a trauma in the late Sixties, after which she began to "SEE WORDS," writ LARGE, on other people's bodies or on surfaces of walls and buildings. What might have been dismissed or narrowly defined as a "psychotic break" by others became for Weiner (already a poet interested in the visual), new material for poems. Conceiving of her page as a screen, she projected in upper- and lowercase "dictation" the speaking voices and seen WORDS appearing from both inside and outside her psyche. In this way she was able to communicate a distressed and chaotic state—with a good deal of humor—as well as constructing a meaningful written artifact containing within it a visualized performance of her daily condition.

In Meredith Stricker's collaboration "The Queen Bee," the erasure or inking-out of the major part of a page from a pre-existing Gothic romance by the same name (fig. 18), poses an utterly different attitude to chaos and reliable language. In an attempt to sift her own immediate and fragmentary message from the predictable detritus of historic language usage, Stricker and her painter friend, Karen Ganz, "draw & paint into a series of books, glue in scraps & pictures to *find/erase* our text" (from a note to author, 1988). Erasing becomes, then, a way of reading and of giving up one's exclusive ownership of the *re*created text. Her "poem" is a study in the discrete selection of syllables and words that deliver absence speaking.

Norma Cole's construction of the poem's syntax is influenced by her spatial experience as a painter, her translator's sense of words as transmutable objects or substitutions. Her notebooks are often composed with handwritten words and bits of found alphabet or images. Figure 19 is from Cole's poem text, "Rosetta" (in *Moira*, 1995). Among the visual pieces she made in approaching the writing of this work, Cole applied—via collage—a photo of her Russian grandmother in Middle Eastern dress to an image of the Rosetta Stone with its three languages. The grandmother, who had emigrated to Canada via Palestine, "became iconic for absence itself," Cole writes. "She was never discussed, or even named to us, until her death. She lived there but was and was not from there" (letter to the author, 1996).

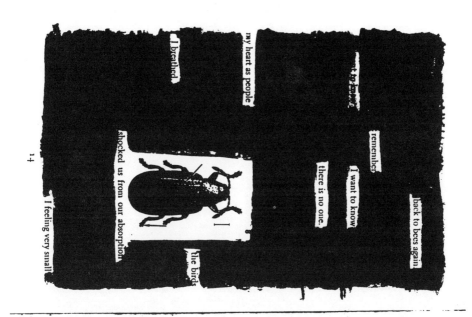

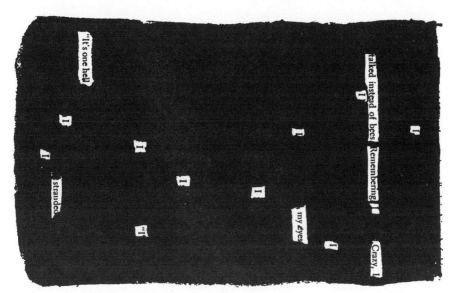

Fig. 18. "The Queen Bee" by Meredith Stricker and Karen Ganz, from *HOW(ever)* 5, no. 1 (1988).

In the "Rosetta" text, Cole composes a language field of three parts which do and do not derive from the same linguistic pulse. In the first section (fig. 19), the § character preceding the first word of each line was

§ear-splitting whistle
undeciphered but proof
of their presence. so he

§deciphered on the level

§ *Courier de l'Egypte*
le 29 fructidor, VII° année
de la République

§the most important of
these 'daughters of Tyre'

§way, path, groove, were those
signs, (mysterious) in their hair

...wave theory of light...the bumpy treatise...we are
...losing...linear ramblings, floors...

                                    its calm flatness...
the broadness and shallowness...

Moving anxiety
        for the reality
moving without you. again
wrapping the proscribed
image in sheets
between
grateful reproductions

Fig. 19. From Norma Cole, "Rosetta," in *Moira* (Oakland: O Books, 1995).

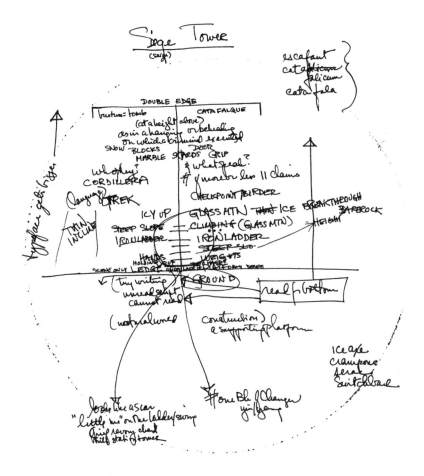

Fig. 20. "Siege Tower" by Catherine Bowers.

chosen from her keyboard precisely because she could attach no meaning, no sound, to it . . . a piece of type, entirely iconic—a translation of something perceived, absent yet elusively there.

"Siege Tower" (fig. 20) is Catherine Bowers' first-draft response to an assignment I suggested to members of her writing group who were asked to find a new scaffolding (poetic structure) for an old obsession (subject matter that clings and will not go away). Bowers had studiously avoided her visual nature, having lived in the shadow of a mother who was a successful painter. She'd determined, instead, to write but was unsatisfied by poems that were well-enough made but leaving out too much of what interested her. Given the invitation to invent a new configuration for her words, she created this first draft to open the field of the page to her suppressed writing impulses.

The second example (fig. 21) is a later poem, marked in its top half by words for color and physicality, deepened in the lower half by a dreamed narrative of the unspeakable.

```
scalpknot/reveal
                                        his dark robes p.23
her fleshpink silk (kimono)      fall open

    carmine lining                      fleshpink inside

      more than one sleight of hand

                    .         .


on the journey my reflections were often melancholy and
when I at last slept I had a dream which I could never
since forget and in which I still see a kind of prophecy


                    .         .
```

Fig. 21. *"scalpknot/reveal"* by Catherine Bowers (unpublished).

Finally, I'd like to look at several poem signatures that extend and celebrate Olson's belief in type's exact placement as carrier of meaning. Mary Margaret Sloan's first published poem, "It Came Up" (*HOW(ever)* 2, no. 2 [1985]) wanted to look like "a fluid surface of juxtapositions and collisions." Ten years later, this example (fig. 22) from her poem "Infiltration" (*The Said Lands, Islands, and Premises*) signals — *within* its high-speed/jump-cut narrative — more awareness of gaps, silences, indecisions *and* "energy flung across synapses."

Thought lines up at clear left and right margins but leaves a moving center of silence—arbitrary spaces to rest in and travel across. Not everything needs to nor can be said. What is uttered into the undetermined and shifting axis hears itself, reflects and moves across the open field to the next fragment, giving us access to the mind's agility, its sensuous diffraction.

```
unloved                       the witnesses whose traces
administer in silence              teaching precaution
need be dreamed as wasted              teaching them
to set fire                      to its natural element
rigged by violence            compositions unearthed
magnetic summons                         glancing off
facts or events                              storage
grotesque but within normal range
                           seeming to want to be alive
to connect nothing                          devising
alarmed                                       states
by force                          with nothing undone
adhering to each                      others' fortunes
                                         were consumed
```

Fig. 22. From Mary Margaret Sloan "Infiltration," in *The Said Lands, Islands, and Premises* (Minneapolis: Chax Press, 1995).

In figure 23, we are looking at two facing pages from Susan Gevirtz's investigative work, *Prosthesis :: Caesarea* (1994), in which the issue of splitting selves (or missing parts of the self)—projection of "the other" (or the other version) onto the page opposite the official version of the text—signals an uncertainty, an act of infiltration into or substitution for the agreed upon version of anything. The author believes in language and in type but finds no stasis. She speaks from the unreliable narrator's shifting perspective, her words reflecting, as if in a mirror, a Rorschach-folded ink profile except that the ink slides along the surface of the opposing page. An original want—or desire—slides into a longer version of itself, as if words changed the second they were committed to paper . . . as if everything were provisional.

Dear ventriloquist,
    You do not know your size   We measure your
intention by the number of witnesses   out loud she is welcome   charges dropped
You are not the assailant   driving the wrong way
down a one way street.   Anything can be turned into a cause
for suspicion   outlaw   actual motion
without   reprimand

the wasting the washing
want   waste   waste wantnt

immersion in hands

Without name there is less to forget
Where the fathers are ashes in the mouth of
the future   Where   in that bend of the road   they still
crouch   knitting and rubbing in an attempt at sense
in the gentle and long the impossible
bandaging of themselves

Fig. 23. Two facing pages from Susan Gevirtz, "Prosthesis," in *Prosthesis :: Caesarea* (Elmwood, Conn.: Potes & Poets Press, 1994).

•

Recent texts by Susan Howe and Barbara Guest bring us back to Olson *and* to that parallel vanguard community of women visual artists whose originating graphic sense made a subtle but pervasive impact on American poetry. Howe, as partisan and primary extender of Olson's pictographic use of type and syllable, has vividly accelerated his imprint (fig. 24).

Guest's trust of the timeless, minimal gesture as locus of the mysterious—its often unnameable presence—proposes a different visual encounter, powerful in what it leaves *un*said, as in a line drawing where the minimal number of strokes may open to immensity (fig. 25). These bodies of work further extend the visual path to new generations of women poets who will find it more natural to em/body space and its tesserae of human utterance.

Magnanimity cannot
in going from one house

naturally
Whose life was spent

Life deceives us

ˣwhat delicate irony
take it to be their privilege
Led I used not to see
GREAT MEN
and birthright to insult me
WITH
THE MANNER OF LIVING
The bark of parchment

NONCOMPATIBLES | So baneful

He could not storm the alphabet of art

bête   x[Bestial ?]

and social weakness

A style so bent on effect and the expense of soul
so far from classic truth and grace
must surely be said to have the note of
PROVINCIALITY

Fig. 24. From Susan Howe, *The Nonconformist's Memorial* (New York: New Directions, 1993).

"a disorder between space and form"

interrupts Modernity

with an aptitude unties

the dissolving string

Fig. 25. From Barbara Guest, *Quill, Solitary APPARITION* (Sausalito: Post-Apollo Press, 1996).

Author's Note: Of necessity, the examples in this essay can provide only a very partial sense of any individual writer's oeuvre and set of influences; nor is there space here to touch on many American, U.K., and Canadian poets whose works might well be part of this discussion. See *Out of Everywhere: Linguistically Innovative Poetry by Women in North America & the U.K.*, edited by Maggie O'Sullivan (London: Reality Street Editions, 1996); and *Moving Borders: Three Decades of Innovative Writing by Women*, edited by Mary Margaret Sloan (Jersey City, N.J.: Talisman House, 1998).

The Uncontainable

Swing and crack of the wrecker's ball. Action. Demolition. I awake with the film running and the image stopped. That absolute moment when volition at once enters and brings down the old building. A structure with its shelter and solidity no longer in place. Necessary rupture and collapse. Then, to see: it's only a building. Only bricks, cement, pipes, wires, and stairs designed for a particular function and statement. Once pinned to someone's drawing board, it had expressed the day "sufficient unto its needs." This architect's drawing—at least for the moment—had been realized. Its articulation and solidity held ground. Claimed territory.

Then, as if to provide the dream's title, the word appears:

DEVOLUTION

a verbal scrim through which to recomprehend the image of destruction. The dream has presented, simultaneously, a photograph and its title, as if in neon, framed large. Webster's defines *devolution* as "a rolling down or falling; the passing (of property, qualities, rights, authority, etc.) from one person to another; *devolve* said of duties, responsibilities, etc.: as, the work *devolves* on the foreman when the superintendent is ill."

FRAME: During the summer of 1996, I spent a week in Boulder at the Naropa Institute, teaching in the "Jack Kerouac School of Disembodied Poetics" program. The writers teaching in that segment were asked to explore various innovative directions in poetry—in workshops, talks, and panel discussions. This talk was presented during that week.

•

Uncertain before these apparently random signs, I am led by the dream's compressed imagery to reading rooms in various local libraries where I spent hours as a child absorbed in the great and not-so-great historic works of literature; texts that had drifted to the surface and remained in sight on the shelves ... out of intention or random neglect. Without knowing it, I was learning very early an order and a hierarchy of literary valuings installed by whatever "superintendent" or "foreman" was empowered to buy the books and keep them in circulation. What were their preferred narratives, and whose working methods best expressed the views and tastes of those empowered to shape our knowledge of language, song, and story? Why did some books remain to represent all poetic language? Why were others removed from the shelf and not replaced? Primary questions for anyone accessing poetic language from an already meticulously mapped grid.

•

You begin from anywhere, nowhere. Language is a private tryst. "No matter how long and elaborate history's procession, the eye meeting it along the muddy road is always first person singular" (Powers 1995).

•

One begins to understand that the established forms one is born into — the well-designed structures that precede, protect, and guide — may limit and even harm the ability to listen for an interior prompt of difference and to follow its peculiar, often "irrational" moves ... having been called *beside the point*. Each writer comes up against this constructed wall and accepts the power, safety, and authority of its limits ... or decides to break through.

•

What would it mean to *listen through* existing written forms? And from such tracking, to revisualize and to reassemble the wall as a page of departure from the known — graffiti of inner drift and disruption, inscribed with the hidden particularity of one still alive.

In the foreword to her twelve volume work, *Pilgrimage*, Dorothy Richardson said that "Phrases began to appear" and "the Stream of Consciousness lyrically led the way" when she allowed herself to listen (1976, 11). The familiar official progression of sentences was replaced by something more spatial, less regimentally sure of itself . . . "a contemplated reality having for the first time in her experience its own say" (10).

·

I do not know what it gives,
a vibration that we cannot name

for there is no name for it;
my patron said, "name it";

I said, I can not name it,
there is no name;

he said,
"invent it."
                    (H.D. 1973, 76)

Why this imperative to find provocative word orders, to invent a visual shape for one's interior life, to distinguish it from all the others who have spoken for it, before it? A bit of personal narrative floats up:

She remembers how, walking away from her only conference with the professor of English literature, she felt confusion and some defeat, sitting across from him at the desk as he returned her new poems, without commenting directly on them, instead explaining to her the abstract idea of poetic form, while drawing for her the image of a wheel with spokes, rim, and center. There seemed to be no fit between what he was saying and what she was hearing in her mind, which, if accurately expressed, would be more like the simultaneous presence of light waves and particles than a wheel . . . a clamor of voices arguing and interrupting, urgent and cacophonous with bits of speech and thought. It occurred to her then that she wanted to try to get that degenerating syntax into a poem, even though the great poems she'd been assigned didn't read like that. She had no idea how she would locate such a counterpoint on the page, but understood that her interior soundtrack while shaped by system was not systematic . . . but interested her for its unacknowledged music. This was 1959. She'd never heard of Apollinaire or Charles Olson, Dorothy Richardson or Gertrude Stein.

•

In Europe, meanwhile, literary history has been gathering—still largely unacknowledged in American classrooms of the late Fifties/early Sixties:
  • Richardson, 1921: "writing as an action and a process" for the purpose of making reading "strange—in syntax, sentence *and* paragraph structure"—rather than writing "in its usual guise of an invisible and omnisciently produced object" (Gevirtz 1996, 26).
  •Woolf, 1929: describes Richardson's new sentence as that "which we might call the psychological sentence of the feminine gender. It is of a more elastic fiber than the old, capable of stretching to the extreme, of suspending the frailest particles, of enveloping the vaguest shapes."
  • H.D., 1926: in naming her novel *Palimpsest*, appropriates the term for her own writing process, seeing herself as temporary host to the guardianship of shared human inscription—the immanence of history, past and present, passing through her as a palpable force . . . poet as conduit, receiver and scribe.
  • Stein, 1926: rejects almost every classbound rule of English language narrative and asserts her obsession with sentences, parts of speech, and grammar's function, predicating the reality of "a continuous present" independent of established syntactical and semantic agreements of meaning.*

These are chapters of Modernism's *devolution*, in which four women—two British and two American—take on the solidity and unabashed authority of existing literary forms and parallel practices by male modernists, to propose their own startling alternatives. Passing from one person to another. Displacing old buildings.

•

---

* In a September 9, 1998, letter to the author, Ulla Dydo stated that "the phrase 'continuous present' is indeed first found in *Composition as Explanation* . . . dates 1926. . . . (You can follow her writing of it in *A Novel of Thank You*.) She rarely used the term later—she didn't theorize more than necessary, even in *Lectures in America* and the later ones."

The poet who turns to language as an active principle cannot simply replicate received forms. She resists standardization and refuses a reverential attitude toward authorial absolutes. The not-yet-articulate in her nags to be acknowledged and expanded beyond pedigreed literary icons referred to as "the forms"—as if all possible formal shapes and cadences had been locked into place, untouchable, disconnected from ever-changing speech use and perceptive field and intellectual event.

Repeating *the known* is acquisitive; it surrenders, as a collector does, to "good things," rather than hazarding uncertain territory; it narrows the range of attentiveness, neglects the unacknowledged.

.

What is this urgency to speak/scrawl/visualize one's moment uncommonly? Given that men and women share the same potential lexicon and a similar modernist perception of social fragmentation, why would a woman poet need to invent her particular versions of it?

"All our daily inclination to be idle tourists, to be comfortable believers, our inclination to tame art or spirit or the unspeakable by *comprehending* it, turns on us. For the uncontainable is everywhere, as Rilke loves to tell us; it is even in ourselves (McHugh 1993, 22)."

Trajectory and barrage, as if to see it on a radar screen, trapping and visualizing the private language still missing from public record. The uncontainable.

One claims the activity of invention through sheer necessity. It is as if you can't help yourself or, conversely, that you are impelled to escape the predictable as it has come to limit your movement—excluding, pre-editing, denying not only nuance and level of perception but *how* one's spirit might move between the inside and the outside. The next opening of the language. The next hands-on structure. As poets were meant to do.

.

"The uncontainable" will not be quieted. It simply needs time enough for dissatisfaction to erupt and a poet of sufficient inventiveness to give it voice. Its propelling impulse has been essential to twentieth-century American prosody. We find it profoundly illustrated in Charles Olson's 1950 manifesto, "Projective Verse" (Allen 1960, 386), where he articulates his physical inability to *fit* into the inherited forms of "closed" verse. Although those forms have inspired other writers, they have not proved to be expansive enough for his own body, his own breath—the energy field that propels his language. He *must* break all visible and invisible restraints and invent a page—a "field"—in which his line, his spoken "energy discharge," can "declare for itself." Reading his essay in the Sixties and reading it now, one is forcibly struck by Olson's ability to listen, recognize, and insist upon the efficacy and necessity of inventing an entirely new system for thinking about language composition. One sees how his concept—so urgently proposed—released immense amounts of poetic energy and invention in his peers, Robert Duncan and Robert Creeley, and in many poets of succeeding generations, each of whom, while developing a unique tonality, proposed (in certain of their own poems) a reading of the page's visual potential and syllabic particularity as demonstrated by Olson.

Almost every great poet has needed to resist the law-abidingness and administrative presence of the superintendent and the foreman, even if the act of resistance is unheralded by theoretical preface. Even the most playful exorcising of grammar and syntax should not be underestimated as a repudiation of traditional guardianship—the refusal of sterile ground—as Stein so steadily demonstrated.

But it *does not matter* to the poet who is just coming into a mature understanding of writing that others have preceded her in their practice of the continuous present, stream of consciousness, field composition, and other named forms of disruptive polyphony. These stand as important companions in the formal recognition of devolutionary necessity. Nevertheless, "No matter how long and elaborate history's procession, the eye meeting it along the muddy road is always first person singular" (Powers 1995).

•

Dorothy Richardson called it "the behind and between," "that dangerous looseness"—the deliberate *in*stability she was importing to a page as vast and ambitious as Olson's. But she believed that women (and, by inference, the woman writer) had been taught to speak within the highly rational confines and grammars of a male-dominant public discourse—that is, "his language." She believed that only by willingly immersing the self in "the miraculous commonplace"—fidelity through attentiveness—could women writers construct a "language" authentically theirs.

"Telling it slant," slide-rule poetics, improvising one's relation to language as often as is necessary, graphics of recursive inquiry, determined & indeterminate cadence. Not to be tamed.

References

Adams, Henry. 1986. *Mont St. Michel and Chartres.* New York: Viking Press.

Allen, Donald. 1960. *The New American Poetry, 1945–1960.* New York: Grove Press.

Auerbach, Nina. 1987. "Engorging the Patriarchy," in *Feminist Issues in Literary Scholarship,* ed. Shari Benstock. Bloomington: University of Indiana Press.

Bates, Milton J. 1985. *Wallace Stevens: A Mythology of Self.* Berkeley: University of California Press.

Benson, Steve. 1981. *Blindspots.* Cambridge, Mass.: Whale Cloth Press.

Bierman, Arthur K. 1973. *The Philosophy of Urban Existence.* Athens, Ohio: Ohio University Press.

Bromige, David. 1980. *My Poetry.* Berkeley: The Figures Press.

Bunting, Basil. 1965. *The First Book of Odes.* London: Fulcrum Press.

————. 1985. *Collected Poems.* Mt. Kisko, N.Y.: Moyer Bell.

Burke, Carolyn. 1985. "Supposed Persons: Modernist Poetry and the Female Subject." *Feminist Studies* 11, no. 1 (Spring).

————. 1997. *Becoming Modern. The Life of Mina Loy.* New York: Farrar, Straus and Giroux, 1996. Paper edition, Berkeley: University of California Press.

————. 1998. "'The economy of passions': Mina Loy and Basil Bunting." *Sulfur* 43 (Fall), 168–73.

Cliff, Michelle. 1978. "Notes on Speechlessness." *Sinister Wisdom* 5 (Winter). Reprinted in Kathleen Fraser and Judy Frankel, eds. *Feminist Poetics: A Consideration of the Female Construction of Language.* San Francisco, Calif.: University Printing Services, San Francisco State University, 1984.

Cole, Norma. 1995. *Moira.* Oakland: O Books.

cummings, e.e. 1958. *A Miscellany.* New York: Argophile Press.

Dahlen, Beverly. 1983. "Notes on Reading Lorine Niedecker." *HOW(ever)* 1, no. 1 (May).

————. 1985. *A Reading 1-7*. San Francisco: Momo's Press.

de Beauvoir, Simone. 1990. *The Second Sex*. New York: Random House/Vintage.

Dickinson, Emily. 1960. *The Collected Poems*. Edited by Thomas H. Johnson. New York: Little, Brown.

Duncan, Robert. 1968. *Bending the Bow*. New York: New Directions.

DuPlessis, Rachel Blau. 1985. "Working Notes," *HOW(ever)* 2, no. 3 (May).

————. 1990. "For the Etruscans." In *The Pink Guitar: Writing as Feminist Practice*. New York: Routledge.

————. 1992. "Lorine Niedecker, The Anonymous: Gender, Class, Genre and Resistances." *Kenyon Review* 14, no. 2.

Eliot, T. S. 1952. *The Complete Poems and Plays, 1909–1950*. New York: Harcourt, Brace.

Faranda, Lisa Pater. 1986. *"Between Your House and Mine": The Letters of Lorine Niedecker to Cid Corman, 1960 to 1970*. Durham: Duke University Press.

Fraser, Kathleen. 1966. *Change of Address*. San Francisco: Kayak Books.

————. 1974. *New Shoes*. New York: Harper & Row.

————. 1980. *EACH NEXT narratives*. Berkeley: The Figures.

————. 1986. *Notes Preceding Trust*. Santa Monica: The Lapis Press.

————. 1993. *When New Time Folds Up*. Minneapolis: Chax.

————. 1995. *WING*. Mill Valley: EM Press.

————. 1997. *il cuore: the heart. Selected Poems, 1970–1995*. Hanover: Wesleyan University Press.

————, and Judy Frankel, eds. 1984. *Feminist Poetics: A Consideration of the Female Construction of Language*. San Francisco, Calif.: University Printing Services, San Francisco State University.

Friedman, Susan Stanford, and Rachel Blau DuPlessis. 1981. "The Sexuality of H.D.'s *Her*," *Montemora* 8.

Gallop, Jane. 1988. *Thinking Through the Body*. New York: Columbia University Press.

García Lorca, Federico. 1955. *Selected Poems*. Edited by Francisco García Lorca and Donald M. Allen. The New Classics series. Norfolk, Conn.: New Directions.

Gevirtz, Susan. 1994. *Prosthesis : : Caesarea*. Elmwood, Conn.: Potes & Poets Press.

————. 1996. *Narrative's Journey. The Fiction and Film Writing of Dorothy Richardson*. New York: Peter Lang.

Gilbert, Sandra, and Susan Gubar, eds. 1985. *The Norton Anthology of Literature by Women: The Tradition in English*. New York: W. W. Norton.

Going, Dale. 1991. *Or Less*. Mill Valley: EM Press.

Grenier, Robert. 1980. *Oakland*. Berkeley: Tuumba.

Guest, Barbara. 1962. *Poems.* New York: Doubleday.

———. 1973. *Moscow Mansions.* New York: The Viking Press.

———. 1978. *Seeking Air. A Novel.* Santa Barbara: Black Sparrow Press. Reprint 1997, Los Angeles: Sun & Moon.

———. 1979. *The Türler Losses.* Montreal: Mansfield Book Mart, M.B.M. Monograph Series.

———. 1989. *Fair Realism.* Los Angeles: Sun & Moon.

———. 1995. *Selected Poems.* Los Angeles: Sun & Moon.

———. 1996. *Quill, Solitary   APPARITION.* Sausalito: Post-Apollo Press.

H.D. (Hilda Doolittle). 1968. *Palimpsest.* Carbondale, Ill.: Southern Illinois University Press.

———. 1973. *Tribute to the Angels.* Part II, *Trilogy.* New York: New Directions.

———. 1974. *Helen in Egypt.* New York: New Directions.

———. 1979. *End to Torment: A Memoir of Ezra Pound.* Edited by Norman Holmes Pearson and Michael King. New York: New Directions.

———. 1983. *Collected Poems.* Edited by Louis M. Martz. New York: New Directions.

Hejinian, Lyn. 1980. *My Life.* Providence: Burning Deck. Revised, enlarged edition, Los Angeles: Sun & Moon, 1987.

Hogue, Cynthia. 1998. "Infectious Ecstasy: Towards a Poetics of Performative Transformation." In *Women Poets of the Americas,* ed. Jacqueline Brogan and Cordelia Candeleria. South Bend, Ind.: University of Notre Dame Press.

Howe, Susan. 1983. *Defenestration of Prague.* New York: The Kulchur Foundation.

———. 1985. *My Emily Dickinson.* Berkeley: North Atlantic Books.

———. 1987. "Where Should the Commander Be." *Writing* 19, no. 5 (November).

———. 1993. *The Nonconformist's Memorial.* New York: New Directions.

Jaffer, Frances. 1985. *Alternate Endings.* San Francisco: HOW(ever) Book Series, 1.

Johnson, Honor. 1984. "Barbara Guest and Lyric Atmospheres," *HOW(ever)* 1, no. 3 (February).

Jones, Amelia. 1991. "The Absence of Body." *M/E/A/N/I/N/G* 9.

Kim, Myung Mi. 1996. *The Bounty.* Minneapolis: Chax Press.

Lakoff, George. 1982. "Continuous Reframing." *Poetics Journal* 1.

Lawrence, D. H. 1950. *Etruscan Places.* Harmondsworth, Middlesex: Penguin.

Loy, Mina. 1982. *The Last Lunar Baedeker.* Edited by Roger L. Conover. Highlands, N.C.: Jargon Society.

McHugh, Heather. 1993. *Broken English.* Hanover: Wesleyan University Press.

Moriarty, Laura. 1996. *Symmetry.* Penngrove, Calif.: Avec Books.

Niedecker, Lorine. 1946. *New Goose.* Prairie City, Ill.: James A. Decker Press.

———. 1968. *North Central.* London: Fulcrum Press.

———. 1985a. *From This Condensery: The Complete Writing of Lorine Niedecker.* Edited by Robert J. Bertholf. Highlands: The Jargon Society.

———. 1985b. *The Granite Pail: The Selected Poems of Lorine Niedecker.* Edited by Cid Corman. San Francisco: North Point Press.

———. 1986. *"Between Your House and Mine": The Letters of Lorine Niedecker to Cid Corman, 1960 to 1970.* Edited by Lisa Pater Faranda. Durham, N.C.: Duke University Press.

———. 1991. *Harpsichord and Salt Fish.* Edited by Jenny Penberthy. Durham: Pig Press.

Olson, Charles. 1983. *The Maximus Poems.* Berkeley: University of California Press.

Owen, Maureen. 1983. "Working Notes." *HOW(ever)* 1, no. 2 (October).

———. 1984. *AE (Amelia Earhart).* San Francisco: Vortex Editions.

Penberthy, Jenny. 1987. "The New Niedecker." *HOW(ever)* 4, no. 1 (April).

———. 1992. "The Revolutionary Word." *West Coast Line* 7 (Spring).

———. 1993. *Niedecker and the Correspondence with Zukofsky, 1931–1970.* New York: Cambridge University Press.

———, ed. 1996. *Lorine Niedecker: Woman and Poet.* Orono, Maine: National Poetry Foundation, University of Maine.

Perelman, Bob. 1981. *Primer.* Berkeley, Calif.: This Press.

Perloff, Marjorie. 1981. *The Poetics of Indeterminacy.* Princeton, N.J.: Princeton University Press.

———. 1986. "Recharging the Canon: Some Reflections on Feminist Poetics and the Avant-garde." *American Poetry Review* 15, no. 4 (July–August).

Pound, Ezra, and Louis Zukofsky. 1981. "Letters, 1928–1930," edited by Barry Ahearn. *Montemora* 8.

Jim Powell. 1990. "Basil Bunting and Mina Loy." *Chicago Review* 37, no. 1 (Winter): 6–25.

Powers, Richard. 1992. *The Goldbug Variations.* New York: Farrar, Strauss and Giroux.

———. 1995. *Galatea 2.2.* New York: Farrar, Strauss and Giroux.

Quartermain, Peter. 1992. *Disjunctive Poetics: From Gertrude Stein and Louis Zukofsky to Susan Howe.* New York: Cambridge University Press.

———. 1996. "Reading Niedecker." In *Lorine Niedecker: Woman and Poet,* edited by Jenny Penberthy. Orono, Maine: National Poetry Foundation, University of Maine.

Richardson, Dorothy. 1976. *Pilgrimage.* Paper reissue, New York: Popular Library.

Rilke, Rainer Maria. 1995. *Ahead of All Parting: The Selected Poetry and Prose of Rainer Maria Rilke.* Translated and edited by Stephen Mitchell. New York: Ingram.

Shange, Ntozake. 1977. *for colored girls who have considered suicide, when the rainbow is enuf.* New York: Macmillan.

Shreiber, Maeera, and Keith Tuma. 1998. *Mina Loy: Woman and Poet.* Orono, Maine: National Poetry Foundation.

Silliman, Ron. 1979. "Notes on the Relation of Theory to Practice." *Paper Air* 2.

———. 1981. "Third Phase Objectivism." *Paideuma* 10, no.1 (Spring).

Sloan, Mary Margaret. 1995. *The Said Lands, Islands, and Premises.* Minneapolis: Chax Press.

Stevens, Wallace. 1961. *The Collected Poems of Wallace Stevens.* New York: Alfred A. Knopf.

Watten, Barrett. 1980. "Russian Formalism & the Present," *Hills* 6/7: 51.

Weiner, Hannah. 1974. *Clairvoyant Journal.* New York: Angel Hair Books.

———. 1982. *Code Poems.* Barrytown, N.Y.: Station Hill (Open Book).

Williams, William Carlos. 1954. *Journey to Love.* New York: McDowell Obolensky.

Woolf, Virginia. 1929. *Women and Writing.* New York: Harcourt and Jovanovich.

———. 1954. *A Writer's Diary.* Edited by Leonard Woolf. New York: Harcourt, Brace.

———. 1959. *Jacob's Room & The Waves.* New York: Harcourt, Brace.

About the Author

Kathleen Fraser is an award-winning poet, prose writer, and the editor/publisher of *HOW(ever)*, a journal of poetry/poetics by women innovators, currently archived on the Web and electronically available in its second series—*HOW2*. Her teaching career began at the Iowa Writers Workshop (1969–71), moving to Reed College (1971–72) and San Francisco State University (1972–92) where, as Professor of Creative Writing, she directed The Poetry Center and founded the American Poetry Archives. Fraser has published extensively, including fourteen poetry collections, prose writings, interviews, and translations from contemporary Italian poets. Her publications include *il cuore: the heart. Selected Poems, 1970–1995* (1997) and *WING* (1995), as well as poems and essays in the recent anthologies: *Moving Borders: Three Decades of Innovative Writing by Women; Postmodern American Poetry: A Norton Anthology; The Art of Practice*; and *Out of Everywhere: Linguistically Innovative Poetry by Women in North America and the UK*. She divides her time between San Francisco and Rome.